Give Me 40 Days

An Invitation for an
Encounter with God

Freeda Bowers

BL BRIDGE
LOGOS

Newberry, Florida 32669

Bridge-Logos

Newberry, Florida 32669 USA
bridgelogos.com

Give Me 40 Days®
By Freeda Bowers

Reprint, 2019

Third Edition, Paperback 2011

International Standard Book Number: 978-1-61036-091-3
Library of Congress Catalog Card Number: 2011935576

Second Edition 2007

International Standard Book Number: 978-0-88270-856-0
Library of Congress Catalog Card Number: 2001086501

Scripture quotations are from the *King James Version* of the Bible.

GIVE ME 40 DAYS is a registered trademark of Freeda Bowers, d/b/a Freeda Bowers Ministries

To my mother,
Gladys Evelyn Alexander,
without whom I would have never
attained the heights in God that I
have known while sitting at
the feet of Jesus.

Mother, I love you.

Endorsements

"A 40-Day guide to prayer and time with God that every Christian needs."

BENNY HINN

❦

"Freeda Bowers is a Godly woman and leader who has learned to listen to God. No matter what your denominational or doctrinal persuasion you will gain inspiration from her special '**40 Days**' with the Lord."

VONETTE BRIGHT (MRS. BILL)
Co-founder, Campus Crusade for Christ

❦

"Freeda Bowers' book, *Give Me 40 Days*, is full of revelation. For all of you who are frustrated, hopeless, discouraged and need a breakthrough, this book is for you. It is full of keys to help change your current situation through tapping into the power of God in **40 Days** of prayer."

CINDY JACOBS
President, Generals of Intercession Ministries

❦

"*Give Me 40 Days* reveals the heart of God and His desire to lead His people into daily intimate communion with promises of great blessings. This 40-day devotional guide will teach you and draw you into an intimate relationship with God."

BOBBIE JEAN MERCK
President, A Great Love, Inc.

❦

"What a precious inspiration to Christians who mean so well yet manage to get themselves so bogged down in responsibilities, duties, good intentions and the work of the ministry. Only God could release you from schedule pressure by adding an additional time frame of prayer into that schedule. What a right word spoken at just the right time."

LIBERTY SAVARD

Table of Contents

My 40 Days Journal

Foreword

*P*rayer is our highest privilege and is a powerful vehicle to usher us into the Holy Presence of God. Unfortunately, in our prayer lives, many believers never get past low gear. We stay in a realm that barely touches the unlimited possibilities that prayer creates, and we rarely move into the realm of the impossible with God.

Now is the season for the Bride of Christ to rise triumphantly and victoriously, and we will only do that as we hear the voice of our Bridegroom, Jesus. To lead us into that place, the Holy Spirit is clearly calling the Body of Christ into higher levels of prayer, constantly wooing her to *"Press toward the mark of the prize of the high calling of God in Christ Jesus"* (PHILIPPIANS 3:14).

It is my pleasure to have personally known Freeda Bowers for over twenty years. I have come to recognize her integrity and perceive her to be a dedicated woman of prayer. This inspired journal is actually a gift to you…a living application of Freeda's testimony and her personal encounter with God. You have in your hands an invitation to accelerate your own transition into the midst of the glory of God.

Most books are meant to be read and put aside, but *Give Me 40 Days* is intended to be a companion on your personal journey into a more intimate relationship with the Lord. This book will meet you right where you are and introduce you to a newfound freedom in prayer.

Few of us pray enough. Often that is because we have never found a plan that is workable in our busy lives. I encourage you to open your hearts to the significance of giving God **40 Days** as Freeda shares with you about this meaningful timeframe given to her by the Lord.

In this book, Freeda gives you a tool to "jump start" a revolution in your prayer life, an essential key to overcoming the cares of this world. If you desire to be more effective and diligent in prayer, I believe that *Give Me 40 Days* is for you.

I trust that this book will forever change your prayer life and inspire you to have hope and faith for great victories in Christ.

Pat Robertson

Acknowledgments

I want to acknowledge many special people for their support in encouraging me to complete this work:

First, to my husband Claud: You have always encouraged me to follow after all that God has put into my heart. Your wisdom and support have been an anchor for me and always a source of great joy. It is my honor to co-labor with you in the work that the Lord has set our hands to. I love and appreciate you.

A sweet note of thanks to our daughter Angela and to our son Victor. Both of you have supported me and my passion to teach the revelation God has given me concerning "**40 Days**." Your encouragement to impart this message to the world has been a constant source of strength. You are both treasures beyond great price to me.

To my son-in-law, Lou: Your steadfastness and ability to stay focused on what is set before you have been great inspirations to me. I deeply admire and respect you.

To Michael Samuel, my first grandchild. I know that only Jesus is perfect, but you must surely be second. You have totally captured my heart and bring me joy beyond measure. With great expectation we waited 40 weeks for you. See, 40 is an important number in your life already. I wanted this whole page to be a huge color picture of you, but my editor said, "NO."

To all of the Partners of WACX-TV: A special thank you for standing with Claud and me in our efforts to bring quality Christian Television to Central Florida. Due to your faithful prayers and financial support, this ministry, which was founded on prayer, has been so fruitful.

It was because of you and praying for your needs many years ago that the Lord gave me the revelation of the "**40 Days**." Whenever you as partners have entered into a "**40 Days**" of prayer with the station, I have rejoiced with you over your amazing praise reports. I highly esteem each of you.

To the Staff of WACX-TV: You have always encouraged me and have served the ministry well. I am honored and humbled to be working in the Master's vineyard with each of you.

To the countless thousands who have watched the SuperChannel over the years: I give you my heartfelt gratitude for allowing me the opportunity to share with you my revelation of the "40 Days." You are dear to me.

To the Board of Directors of WACX-TV and their wives: Sincere thanks to each of you for your many years of faithful support, diligence and guidance. Together we have worked to build the Kingdom of God, and I am so grateful that He put you in our lives.

To my professor at Zoe University, Dr. Judy Fiorentino: You were the first one to encourage me to put the "40 Days" message in print. That was over a decade ago. Okay, so I'm a little slow, but it's finally done. Thank you for planting that initial seed. I am expecting an abundant harvest.

To my sisters, Sharon Johnson and Javetta Saunders: You are both such tremendous blessings in my life. Each

time you gave God "40 Days" and shared with me the results, I was overwhelmed with gratitude, seeing the manifestations of God's unlimited faithfulness in your lives. May we have many more "40 Days" celebrations in the future.

To my brother, Frank McWaters: I am so thankful for you and for your precious relationship with our Lord. I see Him reflected in your life and believe that there are great things yet ahead for you.

To Cumi McKinney: You have been such a model of a true woman of prayer in my life. For over thirty years you have faithfully covered our entire family and the ministry of WACX-TV with prayer. I honor you and call you blessed.

To my assistant, Linda Markowitz: Shalom, my friend. Thank you for your unconditional and everlasting love and patience. You have surely been as a midwife to me in the birthing of this book. Thank you for the hours you have labored with me in prayer as I sought to find the Father's heart. Your faithfulness and determination that this work would come to a righteous completion are genuinely appreciated.

To Linda's husband Lee: Thank you for allowing your bride countless hours away from home as she helped me prepare this book for publication. A homemade 4-layer coconut cake just like your Grandmom Fanny's is on its way to you.

To Bette Strombeck of Koinonia Ministries: Thank you for giving me a platform in Peru, Equator, Bolivia, the Ukraine and Russia to share the message that *Prayer is More Important*. I can still see the many eager faces before me receiving this truth as I taught their hungry hearts.

Beginning with Dr. Larry Keefauver, to the numerous hands that helped with research, editing, layout, graphic design, printing and every other detail necessary to present this book to the Body of Christ: I applaud each of you and present you with a huge bouquet of thanks. This book would still be just a desire of my heart without your tireless efforts. I bless you all.

And most importantly, my deepest gratitude goes to You, Lord. Thank You so much for that midnight whisper, *Prayer is More Important*. Thank You for teaching me how to wait upon You and for helping me understand the significance of giving You "**40 Days**." You are so precious to me. I am open and teachable, Lord. Please show me more.

Introduction

"You can do more than pray
after you have prayed,
But you cannot do more than pray
until you have prayed."

JOHN BUNYAN

Have you ever said, "Lord, something's got to give?" Are life's pressures pushing in and causing you to feel frustrated? Is there not enough of you to go around for family, friends, yourself, your work and, most importantly, for God?

If so, hold on…Don't quit…Don't give up. God is speaking to you just as He did to me. God wants to meet you where you are.

Congratulations on picking up this book. You have made a great choice. You have made a choice that can transform your life … forever! I believe God is about to do a unique and exciting work in your life as you spend **40 Days** with Him.

Yes, this is a 40-Day devotional, but it's not just any devotional. This book is filled with many hope-giving, life-changing nuggets from Scripture and shares with you the story of my first 40-Day journey with God. Throughout the Bible, **40 Days** had a special significance for those who spent **40 Days** with God. Noah, Moses, Elijah and Jonah each spent **40 Days** with God and then conquered despair, won battles, overcame depression, defeated temptation and were filled with hope. Jesus Himself was led by the Holy Spirit to spend **40 Days** in the wilderness with God.

Over and over, I have seen how spending **40 Days** with God has given hope and built faith in thousands of Christians all over America and around the world. Wherever I have traveled sharing this **40 Days** devotional plan for prayer, people have written and called to testify of the wonderful ways God met them in their time of need.

Over the years, God has revealed to me that one of my primary callings in life is to bring people into His presence by delivering hope. I am very excited to tell you that during a period of **40 Days**, you can begin a personal journey of hope that will take you into the presence of the One who loves you the most. Not only will you see God meet your needs, but you will also experience His joy and peace as you abound in hope: "*Now the God of hope fill you with all joy and peace in believing, that ye may abound in hope, through the power of the Holy Ghost*" (ROMANS 15:13).

In the coming pages, I will share with you...

- That spending **40 Days** with God is Biblical, life changing and overflowing with hope.

- How to give God **40 Days**.

- That God will give you the strength, patience, enthusiasm and hope to spend **40 Days** with Him.

- How to pray, study, listen and spend time with God daily.

- What God does with your needs.

- That God also puts the needs of others in your heart.

- How to walk in faith and obedience as you hear God's voice.

- When to do the practical things He has for you each day.

Get ready. You will soon discover that the time you spend with God can redeem the time you thought you needed to accomplish all that must be done. Once again, let me assure you that hope is on the way. No matter how you feel, God's hope is greater than your feelings. God promises to give you all you need: "*But my God shall supply all your need according to his riches in glory by Christ Jesus*" (PHILIPPIANS 4:19).

Now is the time for you to allow God to do His work in you. He urged me to write this book so that you might grow in faith and obedience. God wants you to go from being overwhelmed to overflowing with His presence and power in your life.

Right now you may be crying out, "Lord, something's got to give!" My friend, in your hands is the devotional guide that can open your heart to hearing God's voice and being filled with hope. So, let's get started. God is saying to you, "**Give Me 40 Days**." "*So teach us to number our days, that we may apply our hearts unto wisdom*" (PSALM 90:12).

FREEDA BOWERS

Chapter 1

Lord, Something's Got to Give!

"Prayer is not a substitute for work,
thinking, watching, suffering, or giving;
prayer is a support for all other efforts."

GEORGE BUTTRICK

By 1984 my husband Claud and I had already been in full-time ministry for over six years. God had called us to build a Christian television station in Central Florida, and our ministry was growing quickly. I have always enjoyed accounting and was the head book-keeper for our ministry. Claud was—and still is—the visionary and our chief executive officer. God has given us many natural giftings and talents, and together we make a great team to do the work that He has called us to do.

In 1984 the ministry had not yet acquired a computer, so I spent count-less hours manually entering the deb-its, credits and balances into the accounting journals. This was some-times a tedious and overwhelming task

for me. I had become so consumed in the busyness of doing the natural work that I had failed to let God into the process, and I was on overload.

It was Labor Day weekend that year, and I had taken my ledgers home so I could work on them in the evenings in order to catch up on the financial records. I had also hoped to spend some quality time with my fam-ily, which was why I put aside a good bit of my accounting work until late Monday night.

I was feverishly trying to finish every-thing before retiring to bed. I knew that in a few short hours I would need to go to my designated prayer time at the television station. Every week our faith-ful prayer partners, *Intercessors for Central Florida*, would come individually to the television station to pray for fifty-five minutes for the needs of our viewers and partners and to seek God's guidance for another week of ministry. I was a member of the prayer team, and my assigned prayer time was Tuesdays at 8:00 A.M. Those times of prayer were such precious and awesome divine appointments with the Lord that I always made it a priority to be faithful to my scheduled time.

It was already past midnight when I began a desperately serious conversation with the Lord. All through my life I've had some of the deepest talks with the Lord either very late at night or very early in the morning. These are the times during my day when all external distractions are silenced, and God has my full and undivided attention.

As I contemplated setting the alarm to get up for prayer in a few short hours, I felt that I couldn't pull myself together and go on any longer. I had already spent countless hours on my ledgers, and the work was still undone. At that time I was carrying much of the accounting responsibilities of several different departments in the ministry,

I felt so overwhelmed with all of my responsibilities, both with my family and at the ministry, that I was both physically and emotionally exhausted.

and the realization of my circumstances began to drown me. A riptide of discouragement pulled me down and washed over me like a tidal wave.

I loved God and wanted to serve Him with my whole heart, but it seemed impossible for me to continue. I felt so overwhelmed with all of my responsibilities, both with my family and at the ministry, that I was physically and emotionally exhausted. I genuinely felt that there was no way I could pray for the ministry or for all the prayer needs that had been called in, especially when I had so many needs of my own and such a heavy workload.

With my unfinished ledgers lying before me, I began to argue with the Lord. Have you ever done that? Have you ever intended to pray, but your conversation with the Lord quickly turned from praise to petition and from adoration to argument? In all of my many hours of Bible study, I have never found argument to be an acceptable form of prayer. Nonetheless, arguing was precisely what I was doing. God, in His grace and patience, listened to me in spite of my agitation, physical exhaustion and restless spirit.

In my mind, I cried out to God, "I can't go to prayer in the morning; I have too much to do and no way to do it all." Then sweetly in my spirit I heard the Lord say, *Prayer is More Important.*"

"But," I snapped back quickly, still arguing with the Lord, "not everyone can do the books. Others can pray, but I need to work on the finances. No one else can do my job."

The Lord refused to debate with me. He simply whispered once again, *Prayer is More Important.*" Honestly, I wasn't thrilled with what I heard Him say. In the midst of my telling the Lord how much I had to do, He asked me for more than I thought I could possibly give.

I lacked the energy to pray at all, but God asked me to pray more. I had a multitude of needs, but He asked me to pray for the needs of others. I argued with Him that I needed less to do, but God persuaded me that what I needed was to spend more time with Him.

Then something supernatural happened. I genuinely heard, not just the words the Lord spoke, but I heard His heart. Jesus was wooing me. He was personally inviting me to come and meet with Him. I had a sweet inner witness that His priority for me was to go to my time of intercessory prayer and that something special awaited me there. All of the disagreement left me,

and I committed to go to the prayer room at my regularly scheduled time in the morning.

Before I finally drifted off to sleep, it was settled in my spirit that nothing I could do for the ministry was more important than prayer. Obediently, I set my alarm and went to sleep, gently hearing the Lord say once again, *Prayer is More Important.*"

The next morning, right on schedule, I went to prayer. With a stack of prayer requests in my hand, I entered our prayer room. It was softly lit, painted a soft blue and had plush carpet on which we often knelt to pray before the altar. As I walked in the door, I had already lost sight of the sweetness of the night before and once again felt the despair of my workload overtake me. I was physically there, but only in pure obedience because there was very little faith in me for anything. I can still vividly remember taking those prayer requests and throwing them and watching as they scattered across that ten-foot altar like cards wildly flung from a deck. I kicked off my shoes, looking at all of the needs represented on that altar, and in utter desperation I said, "Lord, something's got to give!" Immediately God spoke to my spirit and said, "**Give Me 40 Days**."

"**40 Days**!" I thought. "Lord, the needs I have You can answer in a week…" but before I had even completed that phrase, I changed it and said, "No, You can meet all of them in a day." Then I nearly chuckled and said, "Lord, You can meet all of my needs right now. You're God!"

The Lord quickly said back to me, "Yes, Freeda, but I have to work through mankind." Again, I heard Him say, "**Give Me 40 Days**."

Those words gripped my spirit and I began thinking, "This must be the voice of God." I knew from my past experiences as a Sunday school teacher that when the Lord speaks to you, His written Word always supports His revealed or proceeding Word. Of course, that doesn't happen when satan speaks. I knew in my heart, and by God's Word, that "**40 Days**" is a Biblical number, and I sensed that God was giving me something very precious and special.

In looking to the Bible, we see that the number 40 is mentioned over 120 times. Some of these references include the following:

- Noah with his family and all the animals, as it rained for **40 Days** (GENESIS 7)

- Moses on Mt. Sinai receiving the Law for **40 Days** (EXODUS 24)

- The spies of Israel spying out the Promised Land for **40 Days** (NUMBERS 13)

- God strengthening Elijah for **40 Days** from one meal (I KINGS 19)

- Jonah preaching repentance to Nineveh for **40 Days** (JONAH 3)

- Jesus being tempted by satan in the wilderness for **40 Days**. (MATTHEW 4)

- Jesus being seen by His disciples for **40 Days** between His resurrection and ascension (ACTS 1)

God began to show me that "40" is a Scriptural number with profound meaning, and I had no doubt concerning this revelation. I was suddenly overcome with a divine energy that literally surged through my body, and I was filled with great faith. I had no idea what to expect in the next **40 Days**, but I knew that it would be something awesome.

God empowered me to gather up those scattered prayer requests, and I began to intercede for each and every need. I was more than capable in God; I felt extremely strong and had renewed strength. My faith was sky-high, and I was filled with hope to go on.

As I remember that pivotal moment several years ago, I can see myself bending in submission to pick up each of those prayer requests. I had such tremendous faith in my heart. I was convinced that this invitation from God was more than simply words in my spirit. I was filled with confidence that God would meet every specific need I had at that time, and Paul's words became a reality to me: *"But my God shall supply all your need according to his riches in glory by Christ Jesus"* (PHILIPPIANS 4:19).

My responsibility that day was not to pray for myself but to intercede for others. Although I had several pressing needs, the needs on those prayer requests became my focus, and the hour just flew by as I submitted myself to that faith-filled time of prayer.

When I walked out of that prayer room, I remember thinking, "I'm the same on the outside as when I walked in, but there is something very different inside my spirit." I felt new freedom and faith surge up from deep within me. I knew that God was going to bless and provide for me, and I was confident that He would help me with my every need. I had done what He asked me to do. I had taken time I felt I didn't have and had drawn on strength I knew wasn't in me in order to pray for others instead of praying for myself and my needs.

That day I began to tangibly expe-

rience Jesus' promise: *"Come unto me, all ye that labour and are heavy laden, and I will give you rest. Take my yoke upon you, and learn of me; for I am meek and lowly in heart: and ye shall find rest unto your souls. For my yoke is easy, and my burden is light"* (MATTHEW 11:28-30).

As you begin your **40 Days**, a critical key for you will be to pray for others. As you do this, God will meet your needs:

"And the Lord turned the captivity of Job, when he prayed for his friends: also the Lord gave Job twice as much as he had before" (JOB 42:10).

"Pray one for another, that ye may be healed" (JAMES 5:16).

During your **40 Days** with God, you can pray for your own needs, but it is vital that you do not neglect to pray for the needs of others. In so doing, you will discover that as you intercede and stand in the place of another, God will pour out His blessings upon you. Petition and intercession are more important than anything you can naturally set your hands to. Don't stop working, but make prayer a priority. God has so wonderfully taught me to arrange my day around my prayer

> *A critical key during your 40 Days will be praying for others. As you pray for others, God will meet your needs.*

time, and not to arrange my prayer time around my personal agenda.

Prayer was More Important than my bookkeeping or balancing the budget. Even though at that time there was no one besides me to work on the general ledger, the Lord wanted me to focus on Him, not focus on serving Him. Jesus desired my trust more than my trying and my abiding more than my accounting. I made a decision to give God **40 Days** and to take my focus away from all my service and tasks.

In bookkeeping by hand, I could spend several hours just locating a single mathematical error. Often when trying to balance the books during those **40 Days**, I thought, "Lord, I just can't do this anymore." Whenever that thought crossed my mind, the memory of hearing God's instruction in that prayer room swept over me again. Once more, there would be a surge of supernatural hope and strength to continue on in Almighty God and keep focused to give Him **40 Days**.

At that time in my life, I probably

Don't stop working, but make prayer a priority. God has so wonderfully taught me to arrange my day around my prayer time, and not to arrange my prayer time around my personal agenda.

had five or six specific needs that were creating great stress and pressure for me. Not one of those needs was super spiritual. Each need was practical and general, but very important to me. During those **40 Days**, instead of going to God with those needs, He led me to pray for the needs of others.

Halfway into that first **40 Days** with God, I sat down and shared with my husband Claud what God had told me in the prayer room that day. I had delayed even telling my husband about my experience so that I could hold the treasure of the **40 Days** close to my heart. Each one of those **40 Days** was a sweet gift from the Lord to me. The Lord's invitation was so very precious; this was a covenant time between Him and me.

Throughout that entire time, God continually confirmed His assurance that He would meet my needs. One by one He took care of those needs without my cries and petitions. I continued to fulfill all of my natural responsibilities while staying focused on the Lord for the entire **40 Days**.

At the time of my first **40 Days** with God, I was already committed to Him. I was a woman of prayer and was very active in my church. But I was stretched and squeezed, and what came out of me was:

- Frustration

- Anger

- Stress

- Guilt

- Feeling overwhelmed

Although I couldn't see it, I was just where God wanted me that day. When I cried out to Him, "Lord, something's got to give," I was in a perfect position to hear everything He wanted to say to me. He had my complete and undivided attention.

I learned more about faith and obedience in those **40 Days** than ever before in my Christian walk. Whenever I thought about praying for myself, God turned my heart toward the needs of others. As I prayed for those needs, God met mine.

At the end of those **40 Days**, my life was changed, not by what I did, but by what God did in me. Actually, I still found myself with much undone at the end of each day. I still haven't figured out how to pack twenty-eight hours worth of "stuff" into a twenty-four-hour day. But God filled every day with patience, assurance and peace. He made my load seem lighter, refreshed my spirit and expanded my faith. Isn't that what you want as well?

This book has been written to help you initiate your own **40 Days** with God. I believe if you will give the Lord this Biblical time period, He can meet your needs, whether they seem insignificant or are so overwhelming that you're nearly crushed beneath their weight. Your faith will also grow in the process as you deepen your relationship with Him.

We always have God's full attention. One of the greatest problems we encounter in prayer is that God seldom has ours. It is my hope that as you read this book, you will commit to dedicate 40 minutes a day for 40 consecutive days, fixing your focus on God. He is a jealous God, and He greatly desires your devoted and undivided attention.

God asked me to give Him **40 Days**. I thought that would be impossible. I was so far behind in my work. I didn't have time to complete my ledgers much less give God **40 Days**! Have you ever been so far behind in your work that you felt you would never catch up? That's exactly how I felt about our financial books in the television ministry. But every time I would get discouraged, I was gently prompted again, "**Give Me 40 Days**."

As my **40 Days** went into the second week of October, I sat back, looked at my work and realized that everything was finished! My quarterly reports were up to date, and I found myself with time to spare. The **40 Days** had passed so quickly, and I was amazed at the way God had sustained me.

As time progressed, I realized I also had renewed physical strength. Looking back and reflecting on that time with more spiritual maturity, I realize that my mindset had helped me make it through that **40 Days**. I had a mindset of faith!

Be careful to realize that your **40 Days** journey will be not only about you but also about your relationship with God. As you dedicate yourself to the needs of others, you will realize how much God delights in meeting your needs.

God's instruction in the prayer room that day hit me hard, but it totally changed my relationship with Him. In addition to being my Lord. He is also my best friend.

I invite you to join me on a spiritual journey for the next **40 Days**. If you decide to dedicate yourself to this journey, I know that you will discover God in a fresh and new way.

In the coming pages, I will share with you how God captured my attention and motivated me to give Him **40 Days**. I dedicated myself to listening *to* Him instead of constantly talking *at* Him. I learned that prayer is a conversation, not a monologue.

Look at your own life and answer these questions:

- Are you feeling like you can't go on the way things are?

- Do you lack the desire to pray?

- Are the little needs in life beginning to overwhelm you and bring you stress?

- Do you find yourself crying out, "Lord, something's got to give"?

- Do you long for a personal encounter with God?

If you could answer *yes* to any of these questions, you are not alone. I have had the opportunity to teach the "**40 Days**" message in many American cities as well as in South America, Israel, the Ukraine and Russia. Whenever I do, I bring the requests of the people back to the television station so that our local prayer partners and I can pray over those needs for **40 Days**. When ministering in non-English speaking nations, I have the people's prayer requests translated into English. I have always been amazed to find that whether those requests come from Florida or the Ukraine, from South Carolina or South America, the needs of the people are often the same.

I have great news for you; the same

God, who faithfully met my needs during my first **40 Days** and continually meets them to this day, can meet yours, too. Consider committing these next **40 Days** to set your focus on your primary, ultimate and most important need, which is meeting with God. Look past your own needs while praying for others, and I believe that you will be amazed at how God takes care of you and meets your needs.

Take a moment right now and listen to God as He says to your spirit, *"Prayer is More Important.* **Give Me 40 Days**."

Do you hear Him?

Chapter 2

Embracing a Mindset
of Faith

*"Our motive for prayer must be the
Divine will, not our own."*

D. LAURENCE SCUPOLI

There are several different reasons to which I credit the victory of the **40 Days** message in my life, but one stands out above all: I had embraced a mindset of faith. Webster's Dictionary defines a mindset as a fixed mental attitude formed by experience or education. I fixed my mind, not on my faith, but on the God of my faith.

Faith will be the key to opening the door to your first **40 Days** with God. Steadfast faith is essential to successfully submitting **40 Days** to the Lord. What is faith? Faith is much more than what you believe about God. Faith is trusting Him fully. Faith is placing your confidence in His voice even when you don't know what to do or where to turn. Faith is standing firm on His Word in the midst of every dif-

ficulty.

A.W. Tozer said that even though the Bible is clear about the importance of faith, outside of a brief fourteen-word definition in Hebrews 11:1, nowhere does the Bible give us an explanation of faith, but it does give us numerous examples of people exercising faith without question.

Many have received powerful personal revelations on faith. One of my favorites comes from Oral Roberts who once said that faith is the power to believe what is right. I decided that I would rather exercise faith than know the definition of it, and I embraced the power to believe what was right. In doing that, I put on a mindset of faith. My entire being was focused on God. When you focus on God, you come to trust Him. When you trust Him, you unconditionally believe that He can do the impossible for you. Such faith builds hope and confidence, both in God and in what He will do in and through you.

What happens when you walk through **40 Days** and beyond with a mindset of faith? For me, whenever satan attacked my thoughts or tried to sow doubt and despair by tempting me to believe that I couldn't keep my commitment, or that I hadn't really heard God in the first place, I simply repeated the awesome invitation the Lord had given me, "**Give Me 40 Days**." Then the Holy Spirit encouraged me: "Now Freeda, it has only been twenty-one days, and I said 40…" Or He would whisper, "It has only been thirty-three days, but I said 40, so why get discouraged? **Give Me 40 Days**."

There were numerous times during my first **40 Days** that I questioned whether or not I had genuinely heard the Lord. I had to keep walking in that mindset of faith, always doing the last thing He told me to do, even when I had not yet seen any results. During times that I was weary in my body and tempted to quit, faith rose up within me, and a refreshing came as I con-

When God spoke to Elijah, He did not speak through the wind, earthquake or fire. He spoke through a quiet whisper.

tinued to stand in faith and obedience. I was pregnant with a great sense of expectancy the entire **40 Days**.

The Lord had told me to give Him that covenant time, yet now, looking back, I see that I tested that voice many times during those **40 Days**. I wanted to be genuinely sure that it was the voice of the Lord I was hearing. He was so gracious to me as He allowed all of my questions and patiently answered every one. God doesn't speak to me in a loud thunderous voice. When He talks to me, it is usually so soft and gentle. I wanted to be absolutely sure that I was hearing from Him.

When God spoke to Elijah in I Kings 19, He did not speak through the wind, earthquake or fire. He spoke through a quiet whisper:

"Go forth, and stand upon the mount before the LORD. And, behold, the LORD passed by, and a great and strong wind rent the mountains, and brake in pieces the rocks before the LORD; but the LORD was not in the wind: and after the wind an earthquake; but the LORD was not in the earthquake: And after the earthquake a fire; but the LORD was not in the fire: and after the fire a still small

voice" (I KINGS 19:11-12).

During your **40 Days**, listen for God's voice. He is always speaking, but you must fine tune how He speaks to you individually. I heard a minister once say that hearing God clearly is somewhat like listening to a radio. The radio tower transmits a signal all the time. If you turned your radio on and nothing happened, you would never think of calling the tower to complain that something was wrong with its signal. Instead, you would check your radio. Is it plugged in? Is it turned on? Is it set on the right channel?

That's exactly how it is with God and us. He is always sending out a signal; we must be plugged in, turned on and set on the channel of what His heart is saying to us. Then we'll hear Him clearly every time.

In prayer, discipline yourself to silence every other voice in your life except the Lord's. Open your spiritual ears and listen for the gentle voice of the Holy Spirit. When He speaks, quickly obey whatever He asks you to do.

As you pray and seek God during your **40 Days**, satan will surely try to tempt you to believe that you are wasting time, especially God's time. Just as some of those around Jesus condemned the woman for wasting expensive perfume by anointing Him (LUKE 7), satan will try to condemn you

for wasting time with the Lord, saying that you should be doing something far more outwardly productive.

The enemy won't have that license if you refuse to focus on yourself. Instead, fix your eyes solely on the need-meeter, Jesus. Do what He tells you to do and say what He leads you to say. Refuse to condemn yourself for not trying to meet all of your needs in your own strength.

During my first **40 Days**, I continually prayed for others and praised the Lord. One need I had, actually the one I considered to be the most important, had not been met on the 39th day. I was about to give up on God ever meeting that need. I was already overwhelmed with gratitude. He had done more than I could have asked or imagined, so that one last thing could be left undone, I thought. But God had other plans. That very day, before lunch, He answered that last need. Isn't that just like God? He waits until you decide that He is most important of all, and then He acts. When we put Him first, He responds to our needs. That's His promise: *"But seek ye first the kingdom of God, and his righteousness; and all these things shall be added unto you"* (MATTHEW 6:33).

On that 39th day I hosted a ladies' luncheon and was so excited to share the amazing things God had done. He had answered my every specific need.

Not one was left unmet, and I still had another whole day to go! Even that last difficult need on my list had been met without me struggling to solve the problem in my own strength. I was overjoyed and filled with faith. God had truly taken care of me.

God Goes Beyond Our Needs

Let me tell you how precious our God is. He is a more-than-enough God: *"Now unto him that is able to do exceedingly abundantly above all that we ask or think..."* (EPHESIANS 3:20). Something surprising happened on my 40th Day. It is just as vivid to me now as it was then. I was walking across my living room when suddenly the thought came to me, "I haven't even asked the Lord to let Angela win the pageant!"

Angela, our daughter, was a sophomore at the local community college. When I began my first **40 Days**, Angela had not yet entered the college's beauty pageant, but now, on my 40th Day, Angela was a contestant, and the pageant was that very night. I simply stopped where I was and prayed, "Lord, will You please let Angela win this pageant for Your glory?" I didn't know then that the Scriptures tell us that all we do is to be done to the glory of God:

"Whether therefore ye eat, or drink, or whatsoever ye do, do all to the glory of God" (I CORINTHIANS 10:31).

Angela is a very outgoing and vivacious young lady, and in my heart I knew that if she won the pageant, it would be a platform for her to share Jesus. She loved the Lord and had no inhibitions sharing about Him every time an opportunity presented itself. Winning the pageant would give her many open doors to share her faith in Jesus.

That night as the pageant progressed, Angela won the honor of being named Miss Congeniality. The contestants themselves vote for this prize. Just before the judges announced the winner, my friend who was sitting next to me leaned over and whispered, "The one who gets this award never wins the title." She was only trying to encourage me in the event Angela wasn't selected. You can imagine how my heart sank in utter despair when Angela was named Miss Congeniality! For a brief moment I wavered, but quickly that surge of faith that had been my constant companion over the past **40 Days** rose up deep within me, and I just smiled and said quietly in my heart, "Thank You again, Lord, for allowing Angela to win this pageant for Your glory."

In a short while Angela was, indeed, announced as the first-place winner. She had worked hard and prepared well. As the former queen placed the crown on Angela's head and presented her with her gifts, I was overjoyed, and my heart was bursting with pride! As you can imagine, my faith was swollen to an overflowing measure. I think I could have walked on water that night. Our beautiful Angela was wearing the crown! God had been so faithful and had given me more than enough. My **40 Days** with the Lord, praying for others and trusting Him, had ended not only with my every specific need met but also with this astounding last minute bonus. Sweetly, Angela did exactly as I had prayed; during her entire reign she continually used her title to share her love for the Lord.

I always like to share this story about Angela when I teach others how to give God **40 Days**. You might have an urgent need arise during your **40 Days**, maybe even on the last day, but don't start over. This is your personal covenant time with God. Don't go back to the beginning because you identify a new need. Keep on going. Keep praise in your heart, and know

For a brief moment I wavered, but quickly that surge of faith that had been my constant companion over the past 40 Days rose up deep within me.

that everything that arises in this season falls under the covering of this precious covenant time.

A Direction of Divine Order

In 1986, Bobbie Jean Merck, a prophetess from Taccoa, Georgia, ministered on the West Coast of Florida and I attended some of her services. After one meeting, she and I had a meal together. I began talking to her about the number 40, and I asked her if she knew what the number 40 meant. Without hesitation Bobbie Jean looked at me intently and said, "Freeda, the number 40 means divine order applied to all earthly things and flesh." Her words leapt in my spirit, and over the years I have embraced that revelation knowledge imparted into my life. I have truly seen God's divine order come into numerous situations that I have prayed for during **40 Days** of prayer. I also have reports from many who testify of the same thing in their own lives.

Cultivating a mindset of faith helps us walk in divine order. Don't look at the **40 Days** you will spend with God in prayer as your own time. They are His divine time, intended to bring His divine order into your life and into the lives of those for whom you are praying. This time is not exclusively for your benefit, even though you will benefit and be blessed. Your **40 Days** are dedicated and consecrated to the Lord. In them He will order your steps and direct your path.

What Are You Seeking?

Your **40 Days** with the Lord is holy. When something is holy, it is set apart and dedicated unto God. Do not feel obligated to hear a specific word from God every day. This is to be a time of liberty, not a time of bondage. In your **40 Days**, your primary focus is to enter into the presence of the Lord, trusting Him for your needs as you pray for the needs of others. If you will purpose to seek His face, you will not be denied: "*When thou saidst, Seek ye my face; my heart said unto thee, Thy face, L*ord*,*

will I seek" (PSALM 27:8).

- Will you make prayer a priority?

- Will you put all of your needs at the feet of Jesus?

- Will you trust Him with every weight and care and give Him **40 Days**?

- Will you seek God's face, expecting a new dimension in your relationship with Him?

- Will you commit to pray for the needs of others?

- Will you abide in faith and obedience to His voice?

- Will you embrace a mindset of faith?

I believe that in prayer and in His Word, you will hear God's voice and know His will. Listen as He speaks to you, "**Give Me 40 Days**."

Chapter 3

Getting Into Position for Your 40 Days

"When we pray for another, it is not an attempt
to alter God's mind toward him.
In prayer we add our will to God's good will...
that in fellowship with Him
We may minister to those whom both
He and we love."

HENRY SLOANE COFFIN

"To everything there is a season, and a time to every purpose under the heaven" (ECCLESIASTES 3:1).

There are set times and sea- sons in the Spirit, and during your **40 Days** it is very important that you be quick to obey the Lord when He speaks. I remember a time that a friend and I were working together wrapping watches that were to be Christmas gifts for some Russian pastors. I felt the Holy Spirit prompt me to give one of those watches to a local pastor friend of mine whom I would see the next day. Instead of quickly preparing to do what I felt prompted to do, I contin- ued wrapping the gifts that were to be sent and completely forgot about set- ting a watch aside to give to my friend.

When I met with my friend the next day, she shared with several of us that she had recently felt led of the Holy Spirit to give her personal watch to someone in need. Immediately, I was reminded of the previous day's prompting. I was deeply convicted and saddened over the fact that I had not prepared the watch as soon as the Holy Spirit had spoken. In my delay to obey, I had missed a wonderful and timely opportunity to be a blessing to this precious friend.

I did ultimately mail the watch, and my friend was blessed with the gift, but I had missed out on the joy of being in God's perfect timing. If I had only been obedient when He had first spoken, it would have been such a witness of God's faithfulness, not only to my friend, but also to all those who were with us that day.

When God speaks, we need to act immediately. Delay almost always causes us to miss the blessing of being a part of God's bigger plan for us and for others. We need to obey His voice as soon as we hear it. In your **40 Days** God may ask you to pray, make a phone call or a visit, give a gift or write a note. Whether the request is big or small, do it cheerfully, and do it immediately.

In obeying God's voice we share in His Kingdom, which is always marked with righteousness, peace and joy. When we walk in obedience to His Word, the Lord gives us peace and joy, and our works are accounted unto us as righteousness. I only want to do righteous works. Everything born out of our flesh will one day be burned as wood, hay and stubble, but God's works will flourish

When God speaks, we need to act immediately. Delay almost always causes us to miss the blessing of being a part of God's bigger plan for us and for others. We need to obey His voice as soon as we hear it.

today and in the age to come.

Redeem the Time

In giving God **40 Days** I have learned great lessons about redemption of time. There are many days when we have so much to do that it seems as if there is no time to give to God. I have found that if I put Him first and am faithful to commit to a prayer time early in the morning, the Lord will often tell me one thing to do that may cut hours of work out of my day.

During my first **40 Days** with the Lord, our son Victor was in high school, and I felt impressed to attend a chorus meeting at the school. I did not want to take the time out of my busy evening to go, but I obediently went; while there I learned about a seamstress who needed work and lived in my neighborhood. Her help with my alterations and mending saved me countless hours of time over the next several years. In my obedience to God He led me to this woman, and the time it took me to go to that meeting was redeemed many times over.

This may seem like a little answer to you, but to a busy working mother and wife this seamstress was truly a gift from God to me.

Another time, I was really burdened about getting so far behind in my office work whenever I had to travel to minister. All of the hours en route to my destination seemed like such wasted time. God inspired me to begin spending some of my travel time in prayer and in listening to teaching tapes and tapes of the Bible. That seemed really simple, but I obediently began doing that. Shortly, I realized that with no extra effort on my part, the office work awaiting me when I returned was being dealt with much more quickly. Again and again God has redeemed my time.

I believe if you will put God first each day, spending time with Him, He will help redeem your time, also. I have learned that if I am too busy to pray, I am too busy. *Prayer is More Important.*

When You Fail to Obey, Repent!

How do you discern if something is not right in your relationship with God? The first key is being sensitive to your inner peace. If you become unsettled and your conscience is no longer at peace, there has been a breach in your relationship with the Lord. Even in the midst of great outer turmoil, the child who is in right relationship with God will have an inner witness of peace.

True inner peace only comes from God. If a deep, abiding peace is missing in your life, repentance is usually necessary.

As you hear God's voice during your **40 Days** and at times fail to obey His instructions, what should you do? You should repent. There is a difference between being sorry and being repentant. Saying you're sorry is a quick, emotional reaction to ease the pain of your guilt. Repentance is a much deeper work of the Spirit. If there is no reversal in your wrongful actions, there has been no true repentance. The Greek word for repent is *metanoia*. It literally means "to change directions, or to reverse and go in an opposite way."

If there is no turning around and moving away from what was wrong, there is no genuine repentance. You may be sorry—sorry for getting caught, or sorry for having to pay the penalty—but being sorry is not repentance.

The starting point for repentance is recognizing and confessing that your sin is against God (PSALM 51:2-4).

These are the steps of true repentance:

1. Confess your sin to God, acknowledging that your sin is against Him (PSALM 51:2-4).

2. Forgive yourself and refuse to allow your heart to condemn you (I JOHN 3:19-24).

3. If you have wounded someone and it is appropriate, go to him or her, ask forgiveness, and be reconciled (MATTHEW 5:23-24).

4. Finally, speak death to the fruit of the crops you have sown with your sinful ways (PROVERBS 18:21).

5. Speak life where death has been present. Ask the Lord to give you a specific Scripture that will sow His life where destruction has been ruling in your life.

The Bible tells us that we can expect to reap what we sow: *"Be not deceived; God is not mocked: for whatsoever a man soweth, that shall he also reap"* (GALATIANS 6:7).

This is a fixed principle of the law of God. When we sin, we plant crops of destruction in our lives. The wages of sin are death, but there is a secondary step that we can take, and I rarely hear teachings about it in the church. Proverbs 18:21 says, *"Death*

and life are in the power of the tongue: and they that love it shall eat the fruit thereof."

Look carefully at that Scripture. There is such great wealth here, and you might miss it completely unless you allow the Holy Spirit to bring its richness to your understanding. Isn't it interesting that the first thing mentioned in this verse is death? God's patterns are always the same. He changes not. First He takes away, and then He gives. The Father required the sacrificial death of Jesus before He gave eternal life. We see the pattern of death first, and then life over and over again in the Bible: *"... He taketh away the first, that he may establish the second"* (HEBREWS 10:9). *"... Except a corn of wheat fall into the ground and die, it abideth alone: but if it die, it bringeth forth much fruit"* (JOHN 12:24).

When you break the law of God, that sin becomes a seed that begins producing a crop of iniquity. You sowed it, and you will surely eat the fruit of it somewhere in your future...UNLESS death comes to that seed. Yield yourself to true repentance and determine in your heart to turn from that sin. Once you've done that,

The wages of sin are death, but there is a secondary step that we can take, and I rarely hear teachings about it in the church.

speak death to the crop of destruction you planted, cutting off its life source before it has the opportunity to bring a harvest of devastation into your life.

By the words of your mouth, you are in total control of your harvests, both evil and good. Speak death and watch the fruits of destruction wither and die; speak life and you will eat life. After repentance, decree a crop failure where you have sinned and sown the wages of death.

This principle of speaking death and life works on both sides. Speak death where you want to see death. Speak life where you want to see life. The power of both death and life are in your tongue.

Speak death and watch the fruits of destruction wither and die; speak life and you will eat life.

Walking in Destiny

Over the years some of satan's greatest attacks on me have been against my physical body. Often when my health was very poor, God would lay the needs of someone else on my heart. Even though I rarely had the strength to do it, I would obediently begin to pray for that person and would perhaps give them a quick call. Time and again I realized after those calls that my health was restored and I was no longer burdened with sickness. Speaking life to others brought the same life to me!

When calling those people, I was functioning in the call of God upon my life of delivering hope. I now realize how walking in my destiny puts me in position to receive life and fullness from the Father. It is so important that you know God's given purpose for your life. When you are in the center of that purpose, there is provision and protection for you that doesn't exist in any other place. For me, delivering hope to others is one thing that drives stress from my body and causes me to walk in health.

Over the years I have allowed stress to destroy much of my physical wellness. Stress is a manifestation of fear and is now recognized by the American Medical Association as an official cause of death. When stress begins to overtake me, I speak death to the roots of fear in my life and I speak life to faith. You cannot operate in fear and faith at the same time. If you are overcome by stress, or any destroyer, remember this death and life principle; it can become the very truth that will set you free.

I have now discovered that I cannot speak about or focus on the physical attacks against my body. Rather, I must speak life over my flesh, pray for others and continue to walk in my purpose. Regardless of how I feel at the moment, I endeavor to deliver hope and speak life to whomever God puts in my path. Embrace this truth for yourself. It will bring wholeness to you as it does to me. It is a higher and better way to live.

With each successive **40 Days** I have given to the Lord, my faith level has grown. There is less and less resistance to the new things of the Spirit because the last thing God did in my life is always so fruitful and brings such joy. Do you need an infusion of God's joy in your life? Is stress overtaking you? Perhaps during your **40 Days** with God you need to ask Him to define for you what your God-given destiny in life is. Knowing that one valuable key will give definition and purpose to your entire life. Aside from your salvation, there is nothing greater than knowing your personal destiny.

Standing in the Gap

Several years ago our son Victor lived about four hours away from home and was looking for a job. He had called, asking for my advice concerning his job search. The only thing that came to my heart at that time was to suggest that I join him in **40 Days** of prayer.

Victor was full of questions: "What does that require? What do you do when you give God **40 Days**?" he asked. I quickly answered, "Well, Victor, we'll set aside **40 Days**, and each day we'll pray and ask God what you need to do."

At that time in his life Victor had no interest in working with us in the ministry. I had no idea what kind of job to pray for, but I had great faith that God would give us His direction for Victor's life if he and I would pray together.

"Okay," Victor agreed reluctantly. "What do I have to do?"

"Well," I suggested, "let's agree to pray forty minutes every day for **40 Days**." Victor was silent on the other end of the phone. Finally, I heard him sigh as he asked, "Oh, is that what I have to do?"

I didn't want to turn him off, so I quietly asked the Lord to give me the right response to that question. The thought came to me to tell him, "Victor, that is what I teach."

Now, I didn't insist that he had to pray forty minutes every day because I knew in my heart that if he would even pray ten minutes a day, it would be more than what he was doing at the time. I simply said, "That is what I teach, Victor." And I left it at that.

Desperate for some kind of a breakthrough, Victor agreed. During that **40 Days**, he called regularly and expectantly, asking, "Mother, has God shown you anything?" Although it was quite unusual for me, the Lord didn't tell me a thing during that entire time; however, we faithfully kept on praying. On the fortieth day, Victor called the television station to talk to Angela and she casually suggested that he come back to Orlando and manage the bookkeeping for Claud's and my personal businesses.

"No," Victor said, "I'd really like to do that, but I could never take someone else's job." He was so discouraged. Because Victor has a very gentle spirit and tender heart, he would never even consider asking us to give him a position that someone else held. Even though we did have a lady doing our personal bookkeeping, Claud would have considered giving Victor that job and pro-

Is stress overtaking you? Perhaps during your 40 Days with God you need to ask Him to define for you what your God-given destiny in life is. Knowing that one valuable key will give definition and purpose to your entire life.

moting her to another position, but that wasn't an option in Victor's mind.

Later that same day an amazing thing happened. Our personal bookkeeper came into my office and gave me her resignation. I didn't know about Angela and Victor's conversation, and I was quite shocked by her decision. "Why?" I asked. She said that several months earlier the Lord had told her that He was moving her on, but for her to wait and that He would give her the exact timing for her resignation. Do you know when that date was? It was on Victor's 40th Day of prayer.

She had no idea that Victor and I were giving God **40 Days**. It was so amazing that she resigned at the very end of that covenant time. God wanted Victor to continue seeking Him all the way through that 40-Day period. Often God will answer me on the third or the tenth day of a 40-Day time with Him, but what He wanted to do was to build Victor's faith through a relationship with Him. When Victor gave

God **40 Days** of prayer, God faithfully gave him the job he needed.

In that **40 Days**, I refused to take on Victor's burden. God was Victor's source, not me. I simply said, "Victor, let's pray. Let's seek God together." As parents, it is important that we seek God for our children's needs, but that we not take on the burden and weight of their cares.

We do our children no favors by constantly bailing them out of difficult times. I didn't "fix it." I just prayed for the Father's will in Victor's life and watched the Lord cause the circumstances to change. God had already established His will for Victor in the spiritual realm, but He didn't reveal that change to us until we spent time with Him.

Victor took that bookkeeping job for a season and is now in full-time ministry with us at the television station.

Do you want God's will for your life? Perhaps you have missed His best for your life because you haven't spent time with Him. It is never too late to hear the heart of the Father for your life.

Time is going to pass anyway. Why not get in communion and agreement with God? Why not submit a covenant time with Him? You have everything to gain and nothing to lose. God longs to fellowship with you. Listen as He says, "**Give Me 40 Days**."

Chapter 4

Starting Your 40 Days

"Prayer is not bending God to my will, but it is bringing my will into conformity with God's will, so that His works may work in and through me."

E. STANLEY JONES

Now is the time for you to seek God. On the following pages you will find a **40 Days** Prayer Guide. I invite you to invest 40 minutes a day for 40 consecutive days to come into a more intimate relationship with the Lord. Before beginning, remember that you must first put on the mindset of faith. There is a vast difference between mere belief, which is important, and belief that is connected with intense expectation. When expectation is present, it produces a corresponding action. That is exactly what James refers to in James 2:17, when he says that faith without works is dead. You will need to put works to your faith, and one of the greatest works I know is to stand in the gap for someone else in need.

A mindset of faith wisely prays according to God's Word and according to His promises. One of God's promises is found in James 5:16. It tells us if we will pray for the needs of others, God will meet our needs.

In over twenty-five years of full-time ministry, I have prayed for thousands of needs. When I pray for the needs of others, I discover that my personal needs get met as well. Choose to invest a part of your **40 Days** into the life of at least one other person. Just as my needs were met the first time I gave God **40 Days**, they continue to be met every time I give Him **40 Days** and stand in the gap for someone who is hurting.

After this chapter you will find a **40 Days** Journal. In the beginning of the journal you will find a place to list your needs and a place to list the needs of others. This is a wonderful opportunity for you to test and to see if God is true to His Word. He's up to the challenge and actually likes it. He longs to open up the windows of heaven on your behalf. I encourage you to heighten your expectation in God, earnestly anticipating His response by committing to pray for someone else as you trust Him to meet your personal needs. Expectation activates your faith, and faith moves God.

As you list your needs, it is important that you be realistic. Reaching in faith without wisdom only sets you up for disappointment. God is the God of miracles, but He is also the God of wisdom. For example, asking Him to help you lose a hundred pounds in your **40 Days** isn't faith; it's presumption, and presumption never produces Godly results. With that kind of mindset you can probably expect to gain weight, not lose. It's much wiser to ask God to give you an easy-to-follow eating plan that will work effectively for you in a natural, healthy and productive way.

On the following journal pages, there are 40 Scriptures—one for each day of your **40 Days**. Along with the daily Scripture, you will find interac-

Expectation activates your faith, and faith moves God.

tive exercises, a prayer and a place to record what the Lord shares with you.

If at all possible, I encourage you to give God the firstfruits of your day. That may mean getting up a little earlier than usual and having your prayer and Bible time before doing anything else. I believe that the Lord's Prayer in Matthew 6:9-13 shows us that the Father intends for us to meet with Him early in the day. Why do I say that? Because in this prayer Jesus teaches us to ask the Father for our daily bread. Are you going to ask for your food for today as you're going to bed?

Jesus also teaches us to ask the Father not to lead us into temptation and to deliver us from evil. How much evil do you get into while you're sound asleep at night? I believe that God wants the firstfruits of our day so He can protect and provide for us, as we need it.

Giving God the first of your day may be hard at first, especially if you're not a morning person, but time and again people who commit the firstfruits of their day to the Lord see Him supernaturally expand the rest of their day. It comes as a supernatural intervention of the Father and is well worth the investment. I have my devotional time in the morning, and God continues to meet me all throughout my day.

Asking a friend to join you in your **40 Days** is a wonderful way to keep you focused. You could commit to pray for their needs and ask them to pray for yours. You would be motivated to keep your friend on track because you would be expecting to benefit from the fruit of their prayers, and they would help keep you on track, too. Teaming up with a praying friend is a great way to give God **40 Days**.

When I set out to write this devotional, it seemed like a monumental task, and I felt that there was no way I could complete it. One day I looked at my assistant and said, "I just need to quit. There is no way I can possibly go through with this."

Her response really encouraged me. She said, "Good! Since you don't think you can do this, the Holy Spirit will have to take over, and it is sure to be a great book." She then continued, "You are destined to do this, Freeda. God has ordained this book from the foundations of the earth, and this is His timing and purpose for you. You can trust Him to help you." She was so positive and supportive that I made a commitment right then to do whatever the Lord wanted, and you are holding in your hand the fruit of that commitment. So again, find a wise, supportive friend with whom you can give God **40 Days**. Together you can

see amazing things manifest on your behalf.

The pattern that God has placed in our hearts at this time is to give Him 40 minutes each day for **40 Days**. In your **40 Days** with Him you can expect to obtain His wisdom and counsel.

"*So teach us to number our days, that we may apply our hearts unto wisdom*" (PSALM 90:12).

40 Days may seem too long, or you may think that even if you were to pray a little that there is no way you could find time to pray for 40 minutes each day. The hardest part is making the commitment, but once that's done, God will enable you to complete it.

Before you begin, simply determine in your heart that you are going to give God 40 consecutive days of prayer. Take your commitment very seriously. Remember, the Bible says that it is better never to make a vow to the Lord than to make one you don't keep. Decide now that you will set aside 40 minutes each day for **40 Days** and refuse to quit once you have begun.

Also, remember that there is no reason to start over if new needs arise during your **40 Days**. Add each one as it comes, just as I did with the situation of Angela's pageant.

This is a special covenant time that you choose to set aside to be with

God and to hear His heart. It is a special time for you to seek Him and to know Him in a special way. Time is going to pass anyway, so why not give the next **40 Days** to God?

When you stay on course, I know you will see a significant change in your life. How can I make such a bold claim? Because there is no way that you can spend such a dedicated time with God and not experience Him in a greater, deeper and more personal way.

Giving God **40 Days**, spending quality time with Him, will cause your understanding of Him and His ways to become very real to you. During your 40 minutes with the Lord each day, I encourage you to give Him time to speak to you. Prayer is a dialogue, not a monologue. Don't fall into the trap of doing all the talking. God longs to share the secrets of His Kingdom with you. To learn those secrets, you must be a good listener.

Also, give God permission to work through you. Ask Him how to pray and what you should pray for. He will lead you to pray specifically.

Finally, and very importantly, determine that your **40 Days** is a covenant time set aside to be in fellowship with your covenant-keeping God and resist all distractions. I rejoice with you in great anticipation of what is to come.

Enjoy your journey. And remember, **Prayer is More Important**.

My 40 Days Journal

❧

"Prayer is More Important"

Give Me 40 Days

Give Me 40 Days—
How more Scriptural could it be,
And will I not answer
Those who seek Me?

What is the greatest need in your life?
It's not too great for Me,
So give Me 40 Days
And the answer you will see.

Read My Word and pray
And I will become larger than the need.
When your eyes look to Me,
I will reveal the answer that's to be.

Those who seek My face
Will hear My voice
For as their God
I am their choice.

And all they need
Will be given by Me
Because to Me
They have bowed their knee.

JESUS

(A writing given by the Holy Spirit
to Karen Hart)

40 Days Journal

Instructions

"The one main concern of the devil is to keep Christians from praying. He fears nothing from prayerless studies, prayerless work and prayerless religion. He laughs at our toil, mocks at our wisdom, but trembles when we pray."

SAMUEL CHADWICK

Now I invite you to join me on a special spiritual journey that will take place over the next **40 Days**. If you will commit yourself to this journey, I know that your prayer life will never be the same. You will discover God in many ways you have never known Him before.

40 Days isn't a long time. It's only six weeks minus two days. So let's get started. Remember, the next **40 Days** are going to pass anyway, so why not give the firstfruits of them to God? As you pursue Him, God will surely draw you closer to Himself and will reveal sweet and precious things to you. He will give you strength beyond your own abil-

ities. He wants to bless you and use you to be a blessing to others. If you will commit to give God 40 minutes a day for **40 Days**, I believe that He will meet you right where you are.

In the place provided, write down your own needs and the needs of those that you will be lifting up in prayer during your **40 Days**. I encourage you to not arbitrarily begin writing down what first comes to your mind but begin with prayer, asking God what needs He wants you to pray about.

Pray for the Father's heart, and He will help you make your lists. God knows better than you what your prayer priorities are. So often we pray out of our desperation or pain, only to fill the room with empty, faithless words. Rarely, do we receive answers from those kinds of prayers. Why is that? It is because we are not praying the will of the Father: "*Thy will be done in earth, as it is in heaven*" (MATTHEW 6:10).

God answers the prayers that are for our ultimate good, not only those that will ease the pain of a momentary crisis. God is not obligated to answer our selfish requests and is more interested in our growth than our comfort.

As you prepare your lists…

- Ask for the Father's heart in every situation you are praying about.
- Listen intently to every instruction of the Holy Spirit.
- Commit yourself to a mindset of faith.
- Discipline yourself to pray 40 minutes every day for 40 consecutive days.

- Pray in a special place where you will be undisturbed.
- Anticipate a glorious covenant time with your Lord.

There are journal pages provided for you each day. I encourage you to write down the following:

- Everything the Lord says to you.
- Every question you have of the Lord.
- Every answered prayer.

I have several completed journals now, and I refer to them often. Each thing the Lord gives me is priceless, and over the years I have learned that there is a greater chance of remembering those wonderful moments with Him if I have them recorded.

I am eagerly expecting wonderful things for you in the days ahead.

Let's begin.

40 Days Journal

Needs List

My Needs	The Needs of Others
• patience w/ my husband	• Rose & Clarence
• Tramaine to get a husband, God to send her a man of God this year.	• Jodie to get a kidney
• my grandchildren (Charity & Leonard) turn their life around + give their life to God.	• Mamie to give God her life
	• Corona virus our World/ Country
• My husbands complete healing	• Sis Lynette (healing) Sis Ashley (healing)
• prayer life	

*If additional needs arise during your **40 Days**, simply add them to the lists above.*

Don't start over: *Remember this is a covenant time between you and the Lord.*

Day 1
Life's Foundation

But seek ye first the kingdom of God,
and his righteousness;
and all these things shall be
added unto you.

MATTHEW 6:33

THIS IS ONE OF THE FOUNDATIONAL SCRIPTURES of my walk with the Lord. I have discovered that the only way I actually obtain the things that I want in the natural is first to pursue the things of the Kingdom of God.

In God's Kingdom, there is only one priority—Jesus Christ. Ask yourself:

Is He your first love? Is your relationship with Jesus the number one priority in your life? If not, Jesus may be your Savior, but He is not your Lord. The word Lord means the same thing in every language of the world. It means boss. It is possible to be a believer in Jesus, and not a follower. True followers of Jesus willfully submit to Him as their "boss." Unless you are a follower of Jesus you will never know the mysteries of His kingdom or enjoy the benefits the kingdom provides.

Jesus will not take second place to anyone or anything else in your life. In the Gospels we see that Jesus taught about His kingdom more than any other subject and in today's verse He tells us that we are to seek His kingdom above all else.

Read the following Scriptures and underline the words that mean the most to you:

When thou saidst, Seek ye my face; my heart said unto thee, Thy face,

LORD, *will I seek.* PSALM 27:8

*Let all those that **seek** thee rejoice and be **glad** in thee: and let such as love thy salvation say continually, Let God be **magnified**.* PSALM 70:4

It is very important during these **40 Days** that you seek the things of God more than you seek the things that you desire. What do you desire most for yourself? Are you willing to lay down your desires and seek the Kingdom of God? Are you willing to lay aside all your wants and fears? Ways that you can seek first the Kingdom of God are as follows (check all those you will commit to today):

- ☐ Giving God the firstfruits of my day.
- ☑ Loving God with all my heart, mind, soul and strength.
- ☑ Obeying the voice of Jesus, the Good Shepherd.
- ☑ Ministering to the needs of others.
- ☑ Praying for others.
- ☑ Meditate on today's Scripture.
- ☑ Other _____

You can trust the Lord. His promises are yes and amen.

For all the promises of God in him are yea, and in him Amen, unto the glory of God by us. II CORINTHIANS 1:20

If the Kingdom of God has not been your chief priority, repent and ask for forgiveness. Ask the Holy Spirit to help you give Jesus and His kingdom the rightful place in your life.

❖ 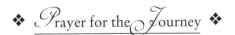 Prayer for the Journey ❖

FATHER, I want You to be my first love and the chief
priority in my life. Today I will seek first
Your Kingdom and Your righteousness
with my whole heart.
In Jesus' name, *Amen.*

The first purpose
of the prayer
is to move
the pray-er.

ROY L. SMITH

Day 1
Life's Foundation

"Prayer is More Important"

I started "Give me 40 Days" March 30, 2020
I want to seek more of God & His kingdom. (Monday)
I'm encouraged to learn" prayer is More Important"
As a christian I've put everything & everybody
before God. Everything seemingly is more
important than my prayer life & my
relationship with God. As a young lady
I always wanted to have a powerful
prayer life but as life got busy I
lost my 1st love.

Day 2
Numbering Our Days

So teach us to number our days,
that we may apply our hearts
unto wisdom.

PSALM 90:12

IN OUR **40 DAYS** WITH GOD, we are numbering our days as a way of dedicating, consecrating and setting aside a sacred, covenant time with the Lord. We set aside dedicated time to Him as a way of showing our love. Just as we spend time with spouses, children, family and friends to express our love for them, so we must spend time with the Lord in order to cultivate our covenant love relationship with Him.

You may show your love for the Lord in many ways. Check any of the ways listed below that apply to you:

I show my love for God by…
- ☐ Worshiping Him.
- ☐ Tithing, giving gifts and offerings.
- ☐ Witnessing to others.
- ☐ Trusting and obeying Him.
- ☐ Being disciplined in prayer and Bible study.
- ☐ Serving Him through ministering to the needs of others.
- ☐ Spending time in His presence.
- ☐ Other _____

When we fail to spend time with the One we love, we miss His will, overlook His ways, misunderstand His voice and disobey His commands. Most of all, when we are not communing with God, we cannot know His heart. The Lord's heart is a heart of wisdom.

There is a vast difference between the wisdom of God and the natural wisdom of man. Read the following Scriptures and note the difference between the two.

I Corinthians 1:19-31 _____

_____

Ephesians 1:17-18 _____

_____

A heart of wisdom desires to see reality through the eyes of God, not through the eyes of man. Wisdom enables us to understand God's ways through being accountable to Him. Wisdom is spending time with God so that we may know what He wants to deposit in us and what He wants to do in us through the power of His Holy Spirit.

If you feel that you lack a heart of wisdom, James 1:5 has a very special promise for you:

If any of you lack wisdom, let him ask of God, that giveth to all men liberally, and upbraideth not; and it shall be given him.

This **40 Days** is a time of accountability. It is a covenant time, a time set apart to minister lovingly to the Lord and to be greatly ministered to by His love.

❖ *Prayer for the Journey* ❖

FATHER, fill me with a hunger for Your wisdom,
so that all I do and say in these next **40 Days**
will come from a heart established in You.
Be my wisdom. In Jesus' name, *Amen.*

*I have been
driven many times
to my knees by
the overwhelming
conviction that
I had nowhere
else to go.*

ABRAHAM LINCOLN

Day 2
Numbering Our Days

JOURNAL

"Prayer is More Important"

_____

_____

_____

_____

_____

_____

_____

_____

_____

_____

_____

_____

_____

Day 3
Salvation in Jesus

That if thou shalt confess with thy mouth
the Lord Jesus, and shalt believe in thine heart
that God hath raised him from the dead,
thou shalt be saved. For with the heart man believeth
unto righteousness; and with the mouth
confession is made unto salvation....
For whosoever shall call upon the name
of the Lord shall be saved.

ROMANS 10:9-10,13

SALVATION IS MORE THAN A HOPE; it is a certainty. You can be confident that you are truly saved from eternal separation from God. He [Jesus] who saves you will not let you go:

The Lord is not slack concerning his promise, as some men count slackness; but is longsuffering to us-ward, not willing that any should perish, but that all should come to repentance. II PETER 3:9

You are so precious to the Lord. Do you know that Jesus would have come to earth and died even if you were the only person He had ever created? Think about that for a moment. You are very valuable to God, and He has a definite purpose for your life.

God does not change, and you can safely rest your confidence in Him. Do you have the full assurance of your salvation? Are you certain of where you will spend eternity? Please check one.

☐ Yes
☐ No

If you checked "yes," then write a prayer of thanksgiving to Jesus for your salvation:

_____

_____

_____

If you checked "no," then please pray this prayer aloud:

> Dear Heavenly Father, I believe that Jesus Christ is your Son and I confess with my mouth and believe in my heart that You have raised Him from the dead. Jesus, I call upon you right now to save me. I give you my life and ask You to take it and do something with it. I invite you into my heart to be my Lord and Savior, now and forever. _Amen._

If in childlike faith you simply choose to believe that the Father has heard and accepted your prayer, you can be certain that you are saved. Your salvation is assured through Christ. He is the author and finisher of your salvation. In Jesus, you are saved from sin, death and hell. You are fully qualified for wholeness and eternal life. Read the following verse aloud:

Neither is there salvation in any other: for there is none other name under heaven given among men, whereby we must be saved. ACTS 4:12

If you have accepted Jesus as your Savior and Lord today, please write to me at the address found on page 227. I would like to hear from you.

❖ _Praise for the Journey_ ❖

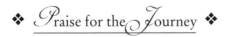

THANK YOU, JESUS, for dying to save me. Make me
a bold witness of Your salvation to others. _Amen._

*Prayer does not
change God,
but changes him
who prays.*

SOREN KIERKEGAARD

Day 3
Salvation in Jesus

JOURNAL

"Prayer is More Important"

_____

_____

_____

_____

_____

_____

_____

_____

_____

_____

_____

_____

_____

Day 4
Righteousness, Peace and Joy in the Holy Ghost

For the kingdom of God is not meat and drink;
but righteousness, and peace, and joy in the Holy Ghost.

ROMANS 14:17

WHAT IS THE KINGDOM OF GOD? It is not an intangible thing that cannot be touched, or felt, or experienced. The Kingdom of God resides within every believer in Christ. It is within you. It is eternal, not temporal. It is for now, not to be put off until later.

The Kingdom of God is not food or drink. How much time and effort do you daily put into taking care of your natural man, doing things like cooking, eating and cleaning up after meals? (Circle one.)

3 hours   4 hours   5 hours   More   Less

Now consider how much time and effort you devote daily to serving God. Even though the majority of our natural hours are dedicated to natural things, our focus and heart priority must always be on the Lord. Is the primary focus of your life on you and your needs, or is it on Him?

The Lord wants you to walk daily in righteousness, peace and joy in the Holy Ghost. Below are some Scriptures that emphasize this. Read each Scripture aloud and hide it in your heart:

Be careful for nothing; but in every thing by prayer and supplication with thanksgiving let your requests be made known unto God. And the peace of God, which passeth all understanding, shall keep your hearts and minds through Christ Jesus. PHILIPPIANS 4:6-7

The Spirit of the Lord GOD is upon me; because the LORD hath anointed me to preach good tidings unto the meek, he hath sent me to bind up the brokenhearted, to proclaim liberty to the captives, and the opening of the prison to them that are bound; to proclaim the acceptable year of the LORD, and the day of vengeance of our God; to comfort all that mourn; to appoint unto them that mourn in Zion, to give unto them beauty for ashes, the oil of joy for mourning, the garment of praise for the spirit of heaviness; that they might be called trees of righteousness, the planting of the LORD, that he might be glorified. ISAIAH 61:1-3*

These things I have spoken unto you, that in me ye might have peace. In the world ye shall have tribulation: but be of good cheer; I have overcome the world. JOHN 16:33

The Holy Ghost will enable and empower you to live in righteousness, peace and joy throughout these **40 Days**. You do not have to exert human effort to attain these things…just trust the Lord and allow the Holy Ghost to be your strength.

❖ *Prayer for the Journey* ❖

FATHER, during these **40 Days**, please fill me with the Holy Ghost so that I might know Your righteousness, peace and joy. Use me as a vessel to bring the fullness of Your Kingdom into the lives of others. In Jesus' name I ask, *Amen.*

Satan trembles
when he sees
the weakest saint
upon his knees.

WILLIAM COWPER
& JOHN NEWTON
HYMN WRITERS

Day 4
Righteousness, Peace and Joy
in the Holy Ghost

JOURNAL

"Prayer is More Important"

_____

_____

_____

_____

_____

_____

_____

_____

_____

_____

_____

_____

_____

_____

*D*ay 5
God's Spirit Dwells in You

But if the Spirit of him that raised up Jesus from the dead
dwell in you, he that raised up Christ from the dead
shall also quicken your mortal bodies
by his Spirit that dwelleth in you.

ROMANS 8:11

*T*HE SPIRIT OF THE LORD IS AVAILABLE TO US, not only for our spiritual needs but also for the needs of our body and soul. He is available, able and willing to quicken our physical, mortal bodies.

List the sick for whom you are praying today. Ask God to save, heal and deliver them.

_____

_____

_____

If you or someone you are praying for need healing in any area of life, stand upon the Word of God. If discouragement sets in, remind satan that the same Spirit that raised Christ from the dead lives in you today and that He will quicken your mortal body. He will bring wholeness and strength.

Read these Scriptures aloud and release your faith to believe them. Circle the phrases that you need to claim.

If thou wilt diligently hearken to the voice of the LORD thy God, and
wilt do that which is right in his sight, and wilt give ear to his command-
ments, and keep all his statutes, I will put none of these diseases upon thee,
which I have brought upon the Egyptians: for I am the LORD that healeth
thee. EXODUS 15:26

Who forgiveth all thine iniquities; who healeth all thy diseases.
PSALM 103:3

He sent his word, and healed them, and delivered them from their destructions. PSALM 107:20

He healeth the broken in heart, and bindeth up their wounds.
PSALM 147:3

But he was wounded for our transgressions, he was bruised for our iniquities: the chastisement of our peace was upon him; and with his stripes we are healed. ISAIAH 53:5

I have seen his ways, and will heal him: I will lead him also, and restore comforts unto him and to his mourners. I create the fruit of the lips; Peace, peace to him that is far off, and to him that is near, saith the LORD; and I will heal him. ISAIAH 57:18-19

The Holy Spirit is the Spirit of resurrection. He will raise the dead to life, and that doesn't refer exclusively to being raised up out of physical death. Especially in sicknesses, such as cancer where a consuming disease has already overtaken a body, resurrection power is necessary. In the natural, there is no way to restore those diseased organs. They must be raised from the dead. Stand on today's Scripture and trust God even for resurrection power, if necessary. It is available to you through a prayer relationship with your Lord. His Word is the Word of life.

❖ *Prayer for the Journey* ❖

LORD, I declare that You are my Healer.
Every need I have I lay before You. I confess with the words
of my mouth and believe in my heart that with Your stripes
I am healed—spirit, soul and body, *Amen.*

*Prayer
is a rising up
and a drawing near
to God in mind
and in heart
and in spirit.*

ALEXANDER WHYTE

Day 5
God's Spirit Dwells in You

"Prayer is More Important"

_____

_____

_____

_____

_____

_____

_____

_____

_____

_____

_____

_____

_____

Day 6
Acts of Faith

What doth it profit, my brethren,
though a man say he hath faith, and have not works?
Can faith save him? If a brother or sister be naked,
and destitute of daily food, and one of you say unto them,
Depart in peace, be ye warmed and filled;
notwithstanding ye give them not those things
which are needful to the body; what doth it profit?
Even so faith, if it hath not works, is dead, being alone.

JAMES 2:14-17

How are you doing at maintaining your mindset of faith? Faith is crucial to the success of this 40 Day journey. Faith is your link to the anointing of God. The anointing is the power of the Holy Spirit that will bring your answers. Your faith will connect you to the anointing, but there is another step. You must add works to your faith. Today's Scripture tells us that faith without works is dead. Like a hand in a glove, faith and works go together. One without the other will stagger and ultimately fall short of God's intended glory.

For example, if you are believing for the salvation of a neighbor but never witness to him, obviously, there is a failing on your part. If you believe God to help you lose weight but refuse to institute any kind of diet or exercise program, the failing is not God's—it's yours. Remember, God works through mankind— and often that is you.

When asking God for help, focus on His Word and on what He is speaking to your heart to believe for, but also ask Him to give you His specific instruction on the works that you need to be applying to your faith. God will sometimes stretch you way beyond your natural comfort zones, often requiring you to do things you don't want to do, and give away the things you cherish most. It is not His intent to deprive you, but to get you beyond having dependence on anything other than Him.

If God requires something that seems sacrificial, I encourage you not to allow your mind to reason away this wonderful opportunity to know Him better. Trust me, there is nothing you can give that is greater than what God will give you in return.

What is God asking you to do right now? Complete these sentences:

For my unsaved loved ones, I am to _____

_____

_____

For my church, I am to _____

_____

_____

For my neighbors, I am to _____

_____

_____

❖ *Prayer for the Journey* ❖

FATHER, I desire to do my part. Show me what I need to do
to cause my faith to be solid and fruitful.
Let me not miss opportunities
to apply works to my faith.
In Jesus' name, *Amen.*

*What am I trying
to get God to do that
I should be doing
myself? Restore a
relationship? Resolve
a problem at work?
Choose my career?
What will I take
responsibility
for today?*

OSWALD CHAMBERS

Day 6
Acts of Faith

"Prayer is More Important"

_____

_____

_____

_____

_____

_____

_____

_____

_____

_____

_____

_____

Day 7
Pray in His Name

And whatsoever ye shall ask in my name,
that will I do, that the Father may be glorified in the Son.
If ye shall ask any thing in my name, I will do it.

JOHN 14:13-14

WHEN YOU PRAY, it is essential that you direct your prayers to the Father in the name of Jesus. This is a very basic and necessary rule of prayer. It is by the name of Jesus, our Mediator, that our prayers are escorted to the Father. If you ask in faith according to His will in Jesus' name, the Father will do whatever you request.

When you pray in the name of Jesus, you invoke the Divine intervention of the One who died that you might have life, and life more abundantly. Jesus is the Word of God. Because the Scriptures are God's will, the Holy Spirit will lead you to pray the specific passages that are needful for your every situation.

Praying in the name of Jesus grants you access into the presence of the Father. In His holy presence every care and concern loses its grip on your emotions. In the presence of God you can expect to find rest in the midst of the most tumultuous times and receive clear instruction on what you need to do next. The name of Jesus is the key that unlocks the door to the presence of the Father. In simple faith just follow the Scripture, exactly how it reads, and believe with your heart that the Father hears you:

Whatsoever ye shall ask of the Father in My name, He may give it you.

JOHN 15:16B.

The power of Jesus' name is demonstrated in each of the following verses (circle how His power is manifested in each verse):

Give Me 40 Days

Then Peter said unto them, Repent, and be baptized every one of you in the name of Jesus Christ for the remission of sins, and ye shall receive the gift of the Holy Ghost. ACTS 2:38

Then Peter said, Silver and gold have I none; but such as I have give I thee: In the name of Jesus Christ of Nazareth rise up and walk. ACTS 3:6

And this did she many days. But Paul, being grieved, turned and said to the spirit, I command thee in the name of Jesus Christ to come out of her. And he came out the same hour. ACTS 16:18

That at the name of Jesus every knee should bow, of things in heaven, and things in earth, and things under the earth; and that every tongue should confess that Jesus Christ is Lord, to the glory of God the Father. PHILIPPIANS 2:10-11

In Jesus' name, prayers are answered; people are saved, healed and delivered. Ultimately, every knee will bow to the One who bears that glorious name. All power in Heaven and Earth is embodied in the holy and precious name of Jesus.

Now, please say with me aloud ... *Jesus, Jesus, Jesus.* Whenever you call upon that name, He immediately responds. I so sweetly remember my grandmother saying, "Freeda, if you are ever in a situation where you don't know how to pray, or if there's no time for long prayers, just say the name of Jesus, and He'll be there." Over the years I have discovered how right she was. Please say it again ... *Jesus, Jesus, Jesus.* Do you feel His presence right now? I do.

❖ 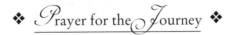 ❖

FATHER, in the name of Your Son Jesus, I ask You
to empower me to submit my entire life to Him.
It is my desire to do and say everything
to His glory, *Amen.*

*When life knocks
you to your knees —
well, that's the best
position in which
to pray, isn't it?*

ETHEL BARRYMORE

Day 7
Pray in His Name

"Prayer is More Important"

_____

_____

_____

_____

_____

_____

_____

_____

_____

_____

_____

_____

_____

Day 8
Satan Will Try to Steal
Your Time With God

There hath no temptation taken you
but such as is common to man: but God is faithful,
who will not suffer you to be tempted above that ye are able;
but will with the temptation also make a way to escape,
that ye may be able to bear it.

I CORINTHIANS 10:13

A COVENANT TIME WITH GOD is detrimental to satan and his entire kingdom. Satan will, indeed, do his part to pull you off track during these **40 Days**. I encourage you at this point to allow no distraction to stop you or any temptation to overtake you.

Check all the things below that tempt you to be distracted from your covenant time with God:

- ☐ Family
- ☐ Work
- ☐ Telephone interruptions
- ☐ Busyness
- ☐ Laziness
- ☐ Internet
- ☐ Hobbies
- ☐ Friends
- ☐ Television
- ☐ Pets
- ☐ Other _____

Distractions are often inevitable. If you are in the midst of your prayer time and are unavoidably interrupted, do not allow the enemy to attack you with condemnation; simply find another opportunity in your day to continue. Your daily 40-minute prayer time does not have to be completed all at once. If you need to pray in segments throughout your day, do that. Just determine not to quit, and I promise you that somewhere in your day, God will give you at least a total of 40 minutes alone to commune with Him.

Not only has God invited you to participate in this **40 Day** encounter with Him, He will give you the grace to complete it. You can confidently trust Him to navigate you through every obstacle and distraction that comes your way. During my first **40 Days** with God I had many opportunities to quit. It seemed as if almost daily something new was added to my schedule and the load I was carrying became greater, but when those distractions came, I took a deep breath and allowed my thoughts to go back to that day in the Prayer Room. Again I would hear the Lord say, "Give Me **40 Days**." Instantly I was refreshed and able to continue on.

Anytime throughout these **40 Days** that you may be tempted to quit, remember today's verse. God has already made a way of escape for you. Ask Him to show you where that escape is. So many times in my life the answer to that question has been so very simple, so simple in fact that I had missed it. I promise you, there is ALWAYS a way of escape.

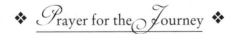

❖ *Prayer for the Journey* ❖

KEEP ME ON TRACK, LORD. Help me to stand firm
on Your promises. Keep my heart and eyes fixed on You.
Remove every distraction that would tempt me
to abandon this covenant time with You.
In Jesus' name, *Amen*.

We are too busy to pray, and so we are too busy to have power. We have a great deal of activity, but we accomplish little; many services but few conversions; much machinery but few results.

R. A. TORREY

Day 8
Satan Will Try to Steal Your Time With God

J O U R N A L

"Prayer is More Important"

_____

_____

_____

_____

_____

_____

_____

_____

_____

_____

_____

_____

Testimonial

I am a diabetic, and in 1991 my doctor told
me that he was going to have to amputate
my leg. I went to a *Divine Appointment*
meeting where Freeda and three other
ministers prayed for me. I had earlier heard
Freeda teach on the message of giving God
40 Days, and I decided to do that,
believing that He would save my leg.
Sometimes, I could only pray 10 minutes at a
time, but I always prayed at least
40 minutes every day. On the 39th day, after
faithfully praying every day, my doctor felt a
pulse in my leg and postponed my surgery.
By 1992 he gave me the report that my leg
was fine and would be saved.

In May of 1999, I fell and broke my right
arm. The orthopedic surgeon told me that
I would never regain full use of that arm
again and that I needed to learn to write with
my left hand. Again, I started on a
40 Days of prayer. On the 40th day I had
a new X-ray, and the arm had healed so completely that the surgeon said that it looked as
if it had never been broken.
The bone and the bone marrow were both in
excellent condition, and there was absolutely
no permanent damage.
The doctor was amazed.

God has been so good to this 82-year-old
grandmother. I can walk—and I can write!

C.W.
Florida

Day 9
Check Your Heart

For the word of God is quick, and powerful,
and sharper than any two-edged sword,
piercing even to the dividing asunder of soul and spirit,
and of the joints and marrow, and is a discerner
of the thoughts and intents of the heart.

HEBREWS 4:12

THE WORD OF GOD IS THE FOUNDATION of our lives, and sometimes a foundation has to be tested in order to verify its strength. These **40 Days** may be a time of testing and trial for you as they were for Jesus in the wilderness, or they may be filled with abundance and overflowing joy as they are for a new mother when her newborn baby arrives. Remember that it takes 40 weeks from conception to delivery for a baby to be born.

Regardless of the direction your journey is taking, I can assure you from my own personal experiences that God has His very best planned for you, and in Him you will ultimately rejoice. I have set aside several 40-Day periods with the Lord since He first asked that of me. Some of those times have been seasons of trial, but none of them outlasted the **40 Days**. Hold fast to your commitment to meet with the Lord during this covenant time, and I promise you that you will see His hand move on your behalf, and on behalf of those for whom you are praying.

I encourage you to check your heart for the possibility that you are praying out of wrong heart motives. Your heart motives reveal who you really are. Even if you can hide your true self from those around you, you can never hide that reality from an all-knowing God. He painstakingly looks upon the intents of your heart as you pray. For example, if you are praying for a son who is on drugs primarily because his behavior is an embarrassment to you, God may withhold your answer until your heart comes into right standing with Him. Without exception, God's first priority is the salvation of your son, not to relieve you of your embarrassment.

Wrong heart motives can sometimes be difficult to identify. A woman once asked me to pray with her for her mother's salvation. The Holy Spirit prompted me to ask this young woman why she wanted her mother saved. She looked at me stunned, hardly believing that I would ask such a question. Because of her shock she was almost unable to respond but finally answered, "Because I don't want her to go to hell!" Now doesn't that sound like a correct answer? I would have thought so too, but the Spirit of the Lord told me to tell her that her heart motive was wrong. He gently said that everything done in the earth is to be done solely for the purpose of bringing glory to God (I CORINTHIANS 10:31). That even means salvation.

For Jesus, **40 Days** in the wilderness brought Him face-to-face with temptation and ushered Him into His ministry on Earth. For Israel, 40 years in the wilderness demonstrated the faithfulness of God. For Noah and his family, **40 Days** within the ark revealed the saving grace of God, even in the midst of judgment. The number 40 in Scripture is a powerful symbol of God working in our lives to accomplish His will. I believe that giving God **40 Days** will bring a mighty intervention of God into your life, too.

During this covenant time, the Word of God will function like a sword in your life to cut away the impure areas of your heart and to remove pride and sin. After the surgery of these **40 Days**, you will experience the healing power of God's presence restoring you and giving you hope.

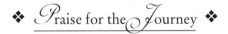

❖ *Praise for the Journey* ❖

FATHER, I praise Your name. With a grateful heart
I thank You for Your Word that is working in my life to keep
my heart motives pure and free from sin and pride. *Amen.*

*In prayer it is
better to have a
heart without words
than words
without heart.*

JOHN BUNYAN

Day 9
Check Your Heart

"Prayer is More Important"

_____

_____

_____

_____

_____

_____

_____

_____

_____

_____

_____

Remember To Record Your Praise Reports.

Day 10
The Power of Forgiveness

And when ye stand praying, forgive,
if ye have aught against any:
that your Father also which is in heaven
may forgive you your trespasses.

MARK 11:25

DO YOU FEEL as though you have had no significant progress in your prayer time? Are you receiving answers to your prayers? If not, I, again, encourage you to check your heart. God desires to give you answers more than you desire to receive them. He is not withholding your answers as a means of punishing you. When things are not going well, a natural weakness of mankind is to look at the shortcomings of others, looking for someone to blame. If you are not receiving answers to your prayer needs, do not look around you, but rather take another look at your own heart.

A major obstacle in your prayer life can be unforgiveness. The sixth chapter of Matthew's Gospel tells us that we cannot expect forgiveness of our own sins if we refuse to forgive others. If you are holding unforgiveness in your heart, it will become a stumbling block in your life that God cannot, and will not, bypass. You must remove it.

Forgiveness is a powerful tool that frees you from the bondage of sin. When God forgives you, you are no longer a slave to sin's captivity. The same is true when you forgive another who you feel doesn't deserve forgiveness. Remember, nothing made you worthy enough for Jesus to suffer and die for you, yet He did. His unending love took Him to a violent death.

Is there anyone in your life that you need to forgive? Ask God to bring to your mind anyone whom you need to release from his sins against you. Then, as an act of your freewill in obedience to God, quickly forgive them. Forgiveness is a choice, not a feeling.

In the heart below, write the names of everyone against whom you are harboring unforgiveness:

Be quick to forgive everyone who offends, wounds, rejects or betrays you so that you might always have free-flowing communication and intimacy with your heavenly Father.

❖ *Prayer for the Journey* ❖

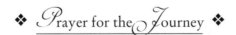

FATHER, I choose to forgive those who have hurt me.
Help me to forgive them even if they never ask my forgiveness.
Please keep me from harboring unforgiveness
in my heart. In Jesus' name, *Amen.*

Lord, help me live
from day to day
In such a self-
forgetful way,
That even when I
kneel to pray,
My prayer shall be
for others.

CHARLES DELUCENA MEIGS

Day 10
The Power of Forgiveness

JOURNAL

"Prayer is More Important"

_____

_____

_____

_____

_____

_____

_____

_____

_____

_____

_____

_____

_____

Day 11
Refuse to Be Offended

And the times of this ignorance God winked at;
but now commandeth all men every where to repent.

ACTS 17:30

A FRIEND WHO HAD ONCE HURT ME deeply came to my remembrance, and I felt the Holy Spirit convict me for being offended by that hurt. Quickly I responded, "But Lord, I have forgiven them. I have forgiven them several times."

Sweetly, the Spirit of God replied, "But Freeda, I never ask you to do what you have already done. I am asking you to repent for having been offended in the first place." Being affected by an offense could have hindered my prayers. Let's see what the Bible says about offense:

And then shall many be offended, and shall betray one another, and shall hate one another. MATTHEW 24:10

Then said he unto the disciples, It is impossible but that offenses will come: but woe unto him, through whom they come! LUKE 17:1

Being easily offended can be detrimental in our walk with the Lord. Look once again at your heart and see if there are yet other offenses in your life. Perhaps you have taken on an offense for someone else. Wives are particularly susceptible to this. When men take a hard blow in the business world, their wives sometimes take that offense upon themselves. Carefully, look at the possibility of this in your own life, and tenaciously guard against the enemy using offense as a weapon against you. Just as importantly, guard yourself against being used as the tool of offense in the life of another.

Make a decision right now not to be offended, and be quick to forgive everyone who has offended you. If you have taken an offense against someone, forgive him or her. If you have caused someone to be offended, repent.

Has the Lord brought anyone new to your mind today that you need to forgive? If so, list him or her here:

_____

_____

_____

At times, even after you have forgiven someone, you may still have uneasy feelings and experience inner turmoil. Ask God to show you if you need to repent. You might need to repent for something you have said. Perhaps you might also need to repent for taking offense for words spoken to you, or for a wrongful action taken against you. The Lord never wants you to take an offense. Perhaps you will need to do as I did and repent for being offended.

❖ *Prayer for the Journey* ❖

FATHER, purify my heart. Expose any foothold
that satan might use against me. Keep me from taking
satan's bait of offense. Teach me how to love
others the way that You love them.
In Jesus' name, *Amen.*

Every time we pray,
our horizon is altered,
our attitude to
things is altered,
not sometimes
but every time,
and the amazing
thing is that
we don't pray more.

OSWALD CHAMBERS

Day 11
Refuse to Be Offended

JOURNAL

"Prayer is More Important"

_____

_____

_____

_____

_____

_____

_____

_____

_____

_____

_____

_____

Day 12
Repentance and Crop Failure

*If we confess our sins, he is faithful and just to forgive us
our sins, and to cleanse us from all unrighteousness.*

I JOHN 1:9

*Death and life are in the power of the tongue:
and they that love it shall eat the fruit thereof.*

PROVERBS 18:21

VERY DAY WE MAY BE TEMPTED TO SIN. Sometimes, it is a
temptation to commit a blatant and deliberate sin; sometimes, we may
be tempted to commit sins of neglect or omission. Psalm 66:18 says, "*If
I regard iniquity in my heart, the Lord will not hear me.*" The word *regard* in
this verse means, "to cherish." If you are actively practicing sin and enjoy the
pleasure of it, and yet are praying for God to manifest on your behalf, you
have no respect or reverential fear of the Almighty Lord of the universe. He will
not hear your prayer, except your prayer to be delivered from that sin.

Is there something in your heart that you truly love and yet know is sin?
You must willingly repent to God for that iniquity and trust Him to help you
be fully delivered from its grip upon your life. As a believer you should daily
confess all of your transgressions to the Lord. Once you have genuinely repented, He is always faithful and just to forgive you of all of your sins.

After repentance you can rest in the assurance that God has removed that
iniquity from your account and that you are in right relationship with Him.
There is, however, a step beyond repentance I would like for you to meditate
upon today. Even though you may be in right standing with the Lord, there is
a fixed principle in the Kingdom of God that says, "*What a man sows, he will
reap*" (GALATIANS 6:7). If you sow bitterness, anger or deception into the life
of another, you can surely expect a harvest of like kind to come up somewhere

82

in your own life. Have you ever heard the saying, "What goes around will come around"? Even the world can identify this fixed principle of the Kingdom of God, but they have no idea how to stop its inevitable cycle of destruction.

Today's verse from Proverbs gives us a powerful treasure from heaven. It is an awesome tool that will enable you to break that destructive cycle of reaping negative crops in your own life. Once you have embraced a Godly sorrow and have genuinely repented of your sin, you have the power in your tongue to speak death to the wrongful crops you planted with that sin. Call for crop failure where you have planted seeds of wickedness, selfishness, deception and perversion.

Today, I encourage you to speak death to the life source of everything evil that is producing bad fruit in your relationships, finances or health, and I believe that you will begin to see a release from much anguish and torment. You can then speak life from the righteousness of Christ that is within you and call forth a harvest of peace and joy.

❖ *Praise for the Journey* ❖

FATHER, thank You for Your faithfulness to me
and for making a way of escape where I have failed.
Thank You for the Blood of Your precious Son, Jesus,
and thank You for entrusting me with the ability
to speak death to the diseased crops in my life.
In Jesus' name. *Amen.*

Don't expect a thousand-dollar answer to a ten-cent prayer.

SUNSHINE MAGAZINE

Day 12
Repentance and Crop Failure

"Prayer is More Important"

_____

_____

_____

_____

_____

_____

_____

_____

_____

_____

_____

_____

_____

Day 13
Surrender Your Expectations

Whether therefore ye eat, or drink, or whatsoever ye do,
do all to the glory of God.

I CORINTHIANS 10:31

MAKE SURE YOUR FOCUS IS CORRECT as you continue through these **40 Days**. As you are seeking God in prayer, reading His Word and meditating on or studying His Word, you should be doing it all to His glory.

Examine the following feelings and emotions (circle any of the following feelings you are having about your **40 Days** right now):

DOUBTFUL	DISAPPOINTED	CONFIDENT
SKEPTICAL	DISCOURAGED	TRUSTING
INSPIRED	FRUSTRATED	HOPEFUL
EXCITED	POSITIVE	JOYFUL
	ANGRY	

If you have negative feelings, your focus has slipped away from giving God glory, and you have, once again, focused on yourself. You have looked more at your circumstances than at your Lord. Remember that you are giving Him this covenant time because He is worthy, not simply because you need something from Him in return.

God will give you your heart's desires when you seek His Kingdom, but to receive is not the primary reason that you pursue Him. Follow after God solely because He is God and He is worthy. Your greatest heart cry during

Give Me 40 Days

these **40 Days** is to offer this time to the Father with the intent of developing an intimate and ongoing relationship with Him.

List three things you would like God to do for you during your **40 Days**:

1. _____

_____

2. _____

_____

3. _____

_____

Are you willing to surrender these expectations? Will you surrender everything to Jesus, including your expectations of receiving from Him during this time? If you will seek Him first, you will prepare an open corridor through which your personal needs can be met. God longs to meet your needs, but He wants to give you those things out of His relationship with you, not apart from it.

❖ *Prayer for the Journey* ❖

FATHER, cleanse me from negative feelings.
Help me to seek first Your Kingdom and an intimate
relationship with You. Keep me from being caught up
in the trap of my own selfish wants.
In Jesus' name, *Amen.*

*If Christians
spent as much time
praying as they
do grumbling,
they would soon
have nothing to
grumble about.*

ANONYMOUS

$\mathcal{D}$ay 13
Surrender Your Expectations

"Prayer is More Important"

_____

_____

_____

_____

_____

_____

_____

_____

_____

_____

_____

_____

_____

_____

_____

Day 14
Christ Is Your Source and Strength

I can do all things through Christ which strengtheneth me.

PHILIPPIANS 4:13

BY OURSELVES WE CAN DO NOTHING. During today's prayer time ask the Lord to strengthen you. He will gladly come alongside and help you in any area you may be weak.

Check the following areas of your life in which you need the strength of Jesus today:
- ☐ Marriage
- ☐ Parenting
- ☐ Work
- ☐ Relationships
- ☐ Finances
- ☐ Health
- ☐ Other _____

Today's verse is very encouraging and one I recommend that you commit to memory. You need to have a treasury of God's promises tucked away in your heart that you can draw upon when you are not near a Bible. Many times I have received strength for my physical body from meditating on today's verse when I have had hours of work that needed to be completed but was so physically tired that I couldn't imagine anything except a nap. I would begin to meditate on these words, "I can do all things through Christ which strengtheneth me." By focusing on these words and allowing them to settle in my heart and mind I would feel revived and refreshed and able to work much longer, and more efficiently than I could have possibly imagined. Jesus IS your strength and He will give you His strength every time you call upon Him in faith.

Read the following Scriptures aloud and underline every phrase that speaks to your heart today:

Rejoice, in the Lord alway: and again I say, Rejoice. PHILIPPIANS 4:4

Be careful for nothing, but in every thing by prayer and supplication with thanksgiving let your requests be made known unto God. And the peace of God, which passeth all understanding, shall keep your hearts and minds through Christ Jesus. Finally, brethren, whatsoever things are true, whatsoever things are honest, whatsoever things are just, whatsoever things are pure, whatsoever things are lovely, whatsoever things are of good report; if there be any virtue, and if there be any praise, think on these things. PHILIPPIANS 4:6-8

Not that I speak in respect of want: for I have learned, in whatsoever state I am, therewith to be content. PHILIPPIANS 4:11

But my God shall supply all your need according to His riches in glory by Christ Jesus. PHILIPPIANS 4:19

Remember that God alone is your source. You can depend upon Him for everything. During these **40 Days** you are not trying to make something happen. You are simply seeking God's will and direction for every area of your life, depending upon His strength and not upon your own. In doing that, I can confidently say that something wonderful will happen for you. The Lord delights in the prosperity of His servants who love Him. If you are faithful, you will not be denied.

❖ *Prayer for the Journey* ❖

FATHER, You alone are the source of my strength
and the direction for my life. Help me to always
keep my life fully surrendered to You.
In Jesus' name, *Amen.*

*Prayer is not only
"the practice
of the presence
of God," it is
the realization
of His presence.*

JOSEPH FORT NEWTON

Day 14
Christic Is Your Source and Strength

JOURNAL

"Prayer is More Important"

_____

_____

_____

_____

_____

_____

_____

_____

_____

_____

_____

Day 15
Faith Comes by Hearing

So then faith cometh by hearing,
and hearing by the Word of God.

ROMANS 10:17

FAITH IS A VITAL KEY in bringing into manifestation the answers to your prayers, and the primary way that faith comes is by hearing the Word of God. As necessary as it is for you to commit yourself to a daily time of prayer, it is equally necessary to spend time daily in your Bible. Using the Scriptures in this devotional guide will be a jumpstart for each day, but I encourage you to increase your daily Bible reading beyond just each daily Scripture.

The way to develop a consistent and ever growing relationship with God is to discipline yourself to spend time with Him. Are you spending 40 minutes each day with Him? If not, I encourage you to commit to that process of discipline for yourself right now. We all have to start somewhere, and it's not too late. Complete each of the following sentences:

- Daily, I will spend _____ minutes in prayer.
- Daily, I will spend _____ minutes in the Word of God.

Since faith cometh by hearing, and hearing by the Word of God, I encourage you to read the Word of God aloud. Research says that we learn by seeing and by hearing. We learn more readily by what we hear than by what we see, but the combination of the two highly increases our retention. It has become very important to me to read the Scriptures aloud.

Read the following Scriptures about faith aloud:

He staggered not at the promise of God through unbelief; but was strong in faith, giving glory to God; and being fully persuaded that, what he had promised, he was able also to perform. And therefore it was imputed to him for righteousness. ROMANS 4:20-22

Therefore being justified by faith, we have peace with God through our Lord Jesus Christ: By whom also we have access by faith into this grace wherein we stand, and rejoice in hope of the glory of God. ROMANS 5:1-2

But what saith it? The word is nigh thee, even in thy mouth, and in thy heart: that is, the word of faith, which we preach; that if thou shalt confess with thy mouth the Lord Jesus, and shalt believe in thine heart that God hath raised him from the dead, thou shalt be saved. For with the heart man believeth unto righteousness; and with the mouth confession is made unto salvation. ROMANS 10:8-10

The best way to build faith in your spirit man is to deposit God's Word into your heart and to meditate upon it throughout the day. Without faith it is impossible to please God (HEBREWS 11:6).

❖ *Prayer for the Journey* ❖

FATHER, during these **40 Days** please enable me
to increase my faith. Please strengthen me in
Your Word and draw me closer to You.
In Jesus' name, *Amen.*

*To pray is the
greatest thing we can
do, and to do
it well, there must
be calmness, time
and deliberation.*

E. M. BOUNDS

Day 15
Faith Comes by Hearing

"Prayer is More Important"

_____

_____

_____

_____

_____

_____

_____

_____

_____

_____

_____

_____

_____

Day 16
Pray the Word

Heaven and earth shall pass away:
but my words shall not pass away.

LUKE 21:33

THE REVEALED WORD OF GOD IS SO IMPORTANT. Often when you have a need, your natural tendency is to pray out of your intellect or current pain. Instead, you should ask the Lord to give you His heart for each need and each situation. After asking for His perfect will, look for a Scripture to confirm what you have heard. God's written Word will always confirm what you hear. Pray the Word, and pray it aloud.

Some Scriptures you may pray aloud include the following:
- Psalm 51 — Repentance
- Numbers 6:24-26 — Blessing
- Psalm 23 — Protection
- Matthew 6:9-13 — The Disciples' Prayer
- I Corinthians 13 — Love
- Proverbs 3:5-6 — Direction
- Psalm 107:28-30 — Deliverance

The Bible says in John 1 that Jesus is the Word. When you pray the Word, you apply Jesus to your need or problem. He is the answer to your every heart cry. Pray the following Scripture prayer, putting your name or the name of someone for whom you are praying in the blanks:

"Bless the LORD, O my soul: and all that is within me, bless His holy name. Bless the LORD, O my soul, and forget not all His benefits:

Who forgiveth all _____'s iniquities;

Who healeth all _____'s diseases;

Who redeemeth _____'s life from destruction;

Who crowneth _____with lovingkindness and tender mercies;

Who satisfieth _____'s mouth with good things;

so that _____'s youth is renewed like the eagle's…"

PSALM 103:1-5

I encourage you to consistently pray the Word of God daily for yourself and for others.

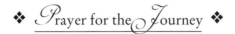

❖ <u>Prayer for the Journey</u> ❖

LORD, please teach me Your Word
and draw me to daily hunger to enter into Your presence
in prayer. May the words of my mouth and the meditation
of my heart be acceptable in Your sight,
O God, my Rock and my Redeemer.
In Jesus' name, *Amen*.

*If you would
have God hear you
when you pray,
you must hear Him
when He speaks.*

THOMAS BENTON BROOKS

Day 16
Pray the Word

"Prayer is More Important"

_____

_____

_____

_____

_____

_____

_____

_____

_____

_____

_____

_____

_____

_____

Testimonial

My husband and I are missionaries in Latin America. We had operated two orphanages there since 1986 and had always rented our facilities. We wanted to purchase our own property but could never find anything that we could afford. Several individuals had been looking for something for us to buy for over eighteen months, with no success.

I went on a **40 Days** of prayer, and within that time we located the perfect house, paid for it in full with the generosity of four donors, and we moved in. It was a true miracle for us. Since then we have never seen another house with as much property for such an incredibly reasonable price. God truly met us in **40 Days**.

We feel that Freeda's teaching on the **40 Days** was a turning point for the churches in Peru, especially relating to their prosperity and intercession. They have given God **40 Days** of prayer several times, each one producing great praise reports. What a tremendous blessing!

B.A.S.
Florida

Day 17
Forgiven and Healed
Through His Blood

But he was wounded for our transgressions,
he was bruised for our iniquities;
the chastisement of our peace was upon him,
and with his stripes we are healed.

ISAIAH 53:5

THE BLOOD OF JESUS paid the price for all of your transgressions, including your sins of omission. Daily each of us sin and fall short of the glory of God (ROMANS 3:23). Below is a cross. Write on the cross the sins that you are being convicted of today. Repent of each one, and thank Jesus that He washed those sins away. Remember also to speak death to any crops you may have planted with the seeds of those sins.

The Word says, *"He was bruised for our iniquity."* One form of iniquity is generational transgression that continues to be passed down from generation to generation. This iniquity may include generational sins such as idolatry, abuse, addiction, perversion and the occult. You may know a family that is trapped with generational bondages such as these. For example, if you know a grandfather, a father and a son within the same family who are all alcoholics, you are most likely seeing a wicked manifestation of generational sin. Generational sin causes generational curses, but there is good news. Through the redeeming Blood of Jesus you can repent for, and be forgiven of all sin, even the sins of your forefathers.*

Remember that… *"the chastisement of our peace was upon him, and with his stripes we are healed."* God wants you healed—spirit, soul and body—and set free. Jesus paid a high price for this freedom.

Because of our sin, Jesus endured merciless beatings, shed His Blood and died that we might be brought into reconciliation with the Father.

In Jesus you have been healed, will be healed and are being healed. How have you experienced His healing power in your life? Briefly complete the sentence below:

Jesus healed me when _____

_____

_____

❖ *Praise for the Journey* ❖
_____

FATHER, I give You praise for Jesus and for His sacrificial
death for me. I thank You for the health I enjoy today, and
I look forward to the day when I will experience a
tangible manifestation of my covenant of health.
In Jesus' name. *Amen.*

*For further information on this subject, see "Generational Repentance" in the resources section at the back of this book.

*Spread out your
petition before God,
and then say,
"Thy will, not mine,
be done."
The sweetest lesson
I have learned in
God's school is
to let the Lord
choose for me.*

D. L. MOODY

Day 17
Forgiven and Healed Through His Blood

"Prayer is More Important"

_____

_____

_____

_____

_____

_____

_____

_____

_____

_____

Remember To Record Your Praise Reports.

Day 18
Waiting Upon the Lord

*But they that wait upon the LORD shall
renew their strength; they shall mount up
with wings as eagles; they shall run,
and not be weary; and they shall walk,
and not faint.*

ISAIAH 40:31

AS YOU WAIT UPON THE LORD and become totally dependent upon Him during this time, He alone will renew you and cause you to mount up on eagles' wings. To become totally dependent upon Jesus, you need to do the following:

TRUST HIM	DELIGHT IN HIM	PRAISE HIM
LOVE HIM	SURRENDER ALL	HEAR HIM
SEEK HIM	FOLLOW HIM	OBEY HIM

Circle those actions that are most difficult for you, and underline those that are the easiest. Ask the Lord to help you today with the areas that you have not totally surrendered to Him.

Read the following Psalm, and repeat aloud those verses that most encourage you to depend upon Him:

Fret not thyself because of evildoers, neither be thou envious against the workers of iniquity. For they shall soon be cut down like the grass, and wither as the green herb. Trust in the LORD, and do good; so shalt thou dwell in the land, and verily thou shalt be fed. Delight thyself also in the LORD; and he shall give thee the desires of thine heart. Commit thy way unto the LORD; trust also in him; and he shall bring it to pass. And he shall bring forth thy righteousness as the light, and thy judgment as the noonday. Rest in the LORD, and wait patiently for him: fret not thyself because of him who prospereth in his way, because of the man who bringeth wicked devices to pass. Cease from anger, and forsake wrath: fret not thyself in any wise to do evil. For evildoers shall be cut off: but those that wait upon the LORD, they shall inherit the earth. PSALM 37:1-8

When you wait upon the Lord, you will be able to run victoriously, not only during these **40 Days**, but also in the months and years ahead. Your job is to wait for His instructions and not struggle to figure things out by yourself. Rest in Him and trust Him to guide you and give you strength.

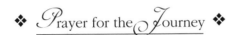

❖ *Prayer for the Journey* ❖

LORD, carry me when I am weak and
teach me how to wait upon You.
In Jesus' name, *Amen*.

*Heaven is full of
answers to prayers
for which no one
ever
bothered to ask.*

BILLY GRAHAM

Day 18
Waiting Upon the Lord

"*Prayer is More Important*"

Day 19
Jesus, the Finisher of Your Faith

Looking unto Jesus the author and finisher of our faith;
who for the joy that was set before him endured the cross,
despising the shame, and is set down at the right hand
of the throne of God.

HEBREWS 12:2

JESUS HAS PLACED faith in the heart of every Christian. The Bible tells us that every believer is given a measure of faith. God never requires something from His children that He doesn't provide. It is our responsibility to nurture our measure of faith.

How is your faith today? Circle the kind of faith you have:

Faith as a mustard seed

If ye have faith as a grain of mustard seed, ye shall say unto this mountain, Remove hence to yonder place; and it shall remove; and nothing shall be impossible unto you. MATTHEW 17:20

Faith that moves mountains

Verily I say unto you, If ye have faith, and doubt not, ye shall not only do this which is done to the fig tree, but also if ye shall say unto this mountain, Be thou removed, and be thou cast into the sea; it shall be done. And all things, whatsoever ye shall ask in prayer, believing, ye shall receive. MATTHEW 21:21-22

Faith to please God

But without faith it is impossible to please him: for he that cometh to God must believe that he is, and that he is a rewarder of them that diligently seek him. HEBREWS 11:6

Faith to see others saved, healed and delivered

And these signs shall follow them that believe; In my name shall they cast out devils; they shall speak with new tongues; they shall take up serpents; and if they drink any deadly thing, it shall not hurt them; they shall lay hands on the sick, and they shall recover. MARK 16:17-18

Jesus has given you your measure of faith, and He is the One Who will finish it. He will give you the ability to look beyond hard times and through difficult places. Jesus was able to endure the anguish of Calvary because He saw the glory that awaited Him on the other side. The cross required that Jesus suffer great pain, shame and separation from His Father. Jesus has been given the authority over all of those things forever. As a joint heir with Him, there is no need for you to live under the bondage of pain, shame, rejection, betrayal or separation ever again. Embrace the faith Jesus has given you, and apply your faith to expect a breakthrough.

❖ Prayer for the Journey ❖

FATHER, during these **40 Days** please undergird my faith
and empower me to trust You in everything I do or say.
Help me to rest in the assurance that You will finish what
has already begun in me. In Jesus' name, *Amen.*

*The penalty of
not praying is the
loss of one's
capacity to pray.*

EDWARD J. FARRELL

Day 19
Jesus, the Finisher
of Your Faith

JOURNAL

"Prayer is More Important"

_____

_____

_____

_____

_____

_____

_____

_____

_____

_____

_____

_____

_____

_____

_____

Day 20
Little by Little

By little and little I will drive them out from before thee,
until thou be increased, and inherit the land.

EXODUS 23:30

CONGRATULATIONS, you are at the halfway point of your **40 Days**! If things are not moving as quickly as you anticipated in the beginning, do not be discouraged. Today's verse is a reminder that sometimes God works little by little. He doesn't withhold things from you as a means of punishment but may orchestrate delays because of His omniscience. He alone knows what you can handle. Every plan God has for your life is for your good. He always knows what is best for you.

When you started this journey of **40 Days**, you felt _____

_____

Now, how do you feel? _____

_____

You can rest in the assurance that Philippians 1:6 gives us:

Being confident of this very thing, that he which hath begun a good work in you will perform it until the day of Jesus Christ.

Entrusting these **40 Days** to God is a good work, and He will enable you to complete it, little by little.

If you are feeling tired or discouraged, release your faith to believe that God's Spirit is encouraging and strengthening you. If you are excited and inspired, rejoice and continue to enjoy the fullness of His abiding presence.

God's desire is always to bless and to encourage you. He drives the things out of your life that are tormenting, harassing, or causing conflict, but He usually does this a little at a time. As you are prepared to manage increased blessings, the Lord will send them to you in abundance so that you might inherit your Promised Land.

List a few things that God has been driving from your life:

1. _____

2. _____

3. _____

If all of the hindrances in your life go at once, God knows that you would have great difficulty holding on to your inheritance. It is very important that you believe God is with you, and that He is always faithful. Even though you may not have yet seen a complete breakthrough in the circumstances you are praying about, little by little God will do a completed work in your life. Don't give up now!

❖ *Praise for the Journey* ❖

LORD, I thank You and trust You for a
complete breakthrough. I know that You
have an amazing inheritance for me, and I rejoice
in what You are doing on my behalf.
I joyfully and gratefully accept Your blessings,
even if they do come to me little by little. *Amen.*

Prayer is not overcoming God's reluctancy; it is laying hold of His highest willingness.

RICHARD CHENEVIX TRENCH

Day 20
Little by Little

JOURNAL

"Prayer is More Important"

_____

_____

_____

_____

_____

_____

_____

_____

_____

_____

_____

_____

_____

Day 21
That Ye Bear Much Fruit

But the fruit of the Spirit is love, joy, peace, longsuffering,
gentleness, goodness, faith, meekness, temperance:
against such there is no law.

GALATIANS 5:22-23

WE MUST CONTINUE to develop a deeper relationship with the Lord. It is only out of a relationship with Him that the fruit of the Holy Spirit can become evident in our lives.

How effectively is the fruit of the Holy Spirit manifesting in your life today? Put an "x" on the line indicating the growth of His fruit in your life:

LOVE

Stagnant | Growing | Mature

JOY

Stagnant | Growing | Mature

PEACE

Stagnant | Growing | Mature

LONGSUFFERING

Stagnant | Growing | Mature

GENTLENESS

Stagnant | Growing | Mature

GOODNESS

Stagnant	Growing	Mature

FAITH

Stagnant	Growing	Mature

MEEKNESS

Stagnant	Growing	Mature

TEMPERANCE
(SELF-CONTROL)

Stagnant	Growing	Mature

The fruit of the Spirit does not manifest in your life simply because you desire it; it comes through a work of the Holy Spirit within your soul. It is important that you be aware of the fruit your life is displaying to others. Are you exhibiting each of the nine fruits of the Spirit in your daily life? Jesus says:

> *Herein is my Father glorified, that ye bear much fruit; so shall ye be my disciples.* JOHN 15:8

❖ *Praise for the Journey* ❖

SPIRIT OF GOD, I thank You for overflowing in my life
in such a way that I can glorify Jesus.
Thank You for using the fruit of my life as an
instrument of blessing to others. *Amen.*

If we are honest, we must admit that much of our time is spent pretending. But when we turn to God in prayer, we must present our real selves, candidly acknowledging our strengths and weaknesses and our total dependence on Him.

ANONYMOUS

Day 21
That Ye Bear Much Fruit

"Prayer is More Important"

_____

_____

_____

_____

_____

_____

_____

_____

_____

_____

_____

_____

_____

Day 22
Sow Good Works

And let us not be weary in well doing:
for in due season we shall reap,
if we faint not.

GALATIANS 6:9

FOR THE NEXT SEVERAL MINUTES read aloud and meditate upon the following Scriptures:

Let love be without dissimulation. Abhor that which is evil; cleave to that which is good. Be kindly affectioned one to another with brotherly love; in honour preferring one another; not slothful in business; fervent in spirit; serving the Lord; rejoicing in hope; patient in tribulation; continuing instant in prayer; distributing to the necessity of saints; given to hospitality. Bless them which persecute you: bless, and curse not. Rejoice with them that do rejoice, and weep with them that weep. Be of the same mind one toward another. Mind not high things, but condescend to men of low estate. Be not wise in your own conceits. Recompense to no man evil for evil. Provide things honest in the sight of all men. If it be possible, as much as lieth in you, live peaceably with all men. Dearly beloved, avenge not yourselves, but rather give place unto wrath: for it is written, Vengeance is mine; I will repay, saith the Lord. Therefore, if thine enemy hunger, feed him; if he thirst, give him drink: for in so doing thou shalt heap coals of fire on his head. ROMANS 12:9-20

Now go back through these Scriptures and underline everything that you feel you can sow into the lives of others today.

As a reminder, this **40 Days** is a covenant time between you and the Lord. It is a season set apart for prayer. I encourage you at this point to resist weariness and refuse to faint in your well doing. Spend some of this covenant time doing deeds of kindness and serving others. Ask the Lord to open doors of opportunity to plant seeds of His love into the life of someone today.

The Bible promises that you will reap if you continue in well doing. The temptation to quit this 40-day journey may be great because the cares of the world will try to pull you aside, but do not lose heart. Decide today to sow some kindness into someone's life. Let your good works so shine before others that they will praise your God in heaven. One of the best ways to get your mind off of your own concerns is to get involved with someone else's need.

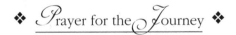

❖ *Prayer for the Journey* ❖

FATHER, keep me diligent in this season of prayer, and
help me to resist the temptation to quit. Please make me
sensitive to someone else in need today.
In Jesus' name, *Amen.*

*Work as if
you were to live
100 years; pray as if
you were to die
tomorrow.*

BENJAMIN FRANKLIN

Day 22
Sow Good Works

JOURNAL

"Prayer is More Important"

_____

_____

_____

_____

_____

_____

_____

_____

_____

_____

_____

_____

_____

Day 23
Give to the Poor

A devout man, and one that feared God with all his house,
which gave much alms to the people, and prayed to God alway.
He saw in a vision evidently about the ninth hour of the day
an angel of God coming in to him, and saying unto him,
Cornelius. And when he looked on him, he was afraid,
and said, What is it, Lord? And he said unto him,
Thy prayers and thine alms are come up
for a memorial before God.

ACTS 10:2-4

CORNELIUS WAS A MAN OF PRAYER, who gave much in alms. Alms are anything freely given to relieve the plight of the poor, expecting nothing in return. The Scriptures tell us that Cornelius' prayers and alms had come up as a memorial before God.

For whom are you praying?

_____

_____

To whom are you giving?

_____

_____

Prayer and giving are inseparable. Ask the Lord to bring someone across your path that you can give something to as a memorial to Him. When you meet that person, minister to him with a heart of love, doing everything in your ability to meet his need.

He that hath pity upon the poor lendeth unto the LORD; and that which he hath given will he pay him again. PROVERBS 19:17

Give Me 40 Days

The word poor does not refer exclusively to the lack of money or possessions. It can also refer to other needs of a person, such as health, kindness, friendship, etc. There are many things you can give besides money that will be an investment of the Kingdom into someone else's life.

Underline in the following verses what we are to give to others:

Then shall the King say unto them on his right hand, Come, ye blessed of my Father, inherit the kingdom prepared for you from the foundation of the world: For I was hungry, and ye gave me meat: I was thirsty, and ye gave me drink: I was a stranger, and ye took me in: Naked, and ye clothed me: I was sick, and ye visited me: I was in prison, and ye came unto me. Then shall the righteous answer him, saying, Lord, when saw we thee hungry, and fed thee? or thirsty, and gave thee drink? When saw we thee a stranger, and took thee in? or naked, and clothed thee? Or when saw we thee sick, or in prison, and came unto thee? And the King shall answer and say unto them, Verily I say unto you, Inasmuch as ye have done it unto one of the least of these my brethren, ye have done it unto me. MATTHEW 25:34-40

Be sensitive to the needs of those that the Lord brings into your path. Be keenly aware of the opportunities He provides for you to be a blessing. Sometimes, that means nothing more than giving a smile, babysitting for a busy mother or helping the elderly or disabled load groceries into their car. If you will be tender and open, God will give you many opportunities to bring up a pleasing memorial before Him.

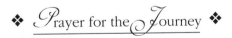

❖ *Prayer for the Journey* ❖

FATHER, show me a person into whose life I can
sow a memorial unto You. Help me to give cheerfully
and generously to the poor. In Jesus' name, *Amen.*

Prayer is not a means by which we get something for ourselves, but rather a method of helping God get something for Himself.

KATHYRN KUHLMAN

Day 23
Give to the Poor

J O U R N A L

"Prayer is More Important"

_____

_____

_____

_____

_____

_____

_____

_____

_____

_____

_____

_____

_____

Day 24
Don't Take on the Burdens of Others

For it is God which worketh in you both
to will and to do of his good pleasure. Do all things
without murmurings and disputings.

PHILIPPIANS 2:13-14

AT TIMES WE ARE TEMPTED to take on the burdens of others, but we simply cannot do that. Today's Scripture instructs us to do all things without murmuring, complaining and disputing. One thing that causes murmuring is carrying the weight of someone else's cares and burdens.

When you sow into the lives of others and still have needs in your own life, you may be tempted to complain. The first time I gave God **40 Days**, I had so many personal cares that I had difficulty even noticing the needs of others. At times, even the needs of our ministry and the concerns of my family became a burden for me.

God does not call you to take on the burdens of others, only to pray for them. But what happens to their burdens? Your prayers cause God to send divine intervention to ease their load. Read the following verses aloud, and then underline what God says to do with your cares and burdens:

Come unto me, all ye that labour and are heavy laden, and I will give you rest. Take my yoke upon you, and learn of me; for I am meek and lowly in heart: and ye shall find rest unto your souls. For my yoke is easy, and my burden is light. MATTHEW 11:28-30

I remember during that first **40 Days** of prayer, I occasionally got discouraged, but my faith remained strong because of the Lord's presence. Whenever I was tempted to be drawn into despair, my mind would go right back to my encounter with God in the prayer room, and I, once again, heard the Lord say, "**Give Me 40 Days**." His voice was so assuring, and I knew in my heart that I could continue with Him in that precious covenant time.

I encourage you to resist all temptation to take on the burdens of others. If you are weighted down in discouragement on the behalf of another, cast that care upon the Lord, and stay on track. Stay focused on what God has called you to do. Get into your Bible, and listen to what He is saying to you personally.

Avoid all temptation to murmur. Remember that murmuring kept Israel in the wilderness for 40 years! If you are murmuring and disputing, you are in absolute disobedience. If you are in disobedience, you cannot be in faith, and without faith you cannot see the answers to your prayers. These are all pitfalls that the enemy sets before us. If we know of his plans in advance, we are far less likely to fall into his traps.

Complete these sentences:

I am tempted to complain about _____

_____

I am tempted to become discouraged when _____

_____

What helps me stop murmuring is _____

_____

❖ *Prayer for the Journey* ❖

LORD, please remove all murmuring and complaining from my lips.
Encourage me with Your strength and Your hope so that with
a pure heart I may encourage and bless others.
In Jesus' name, *Amen.*

*Prayer is not
learned by rote;
it is experienced.
Just talk and listen.
It's no more
difficult than that.*

A.W. TOZER

Day 24
Don't Take on the
Burdens of Others

J O U R N A L

"Prayer is More Important"

_____

_____

_____

_____

_____

_____

_____

_____

_____

_____

_____

_____

Testimonial

Following are four testimonials
from our congregation that came as a result
of our most recent **40 Days** of prayer.

SYLVIA CAMACHA DE SALCEDO
Ekklesia Church, Bolivia

I asked God to make it possible
for us to get authorization from
the government to build a construction.
We had been waiting five years
for permission, and God granted our prayer.
We now have our permit.

N.M.

I play the keyboard for several church meetings
and needed a new keyboard. Many of the keys
on the one I was using would stick or not play at all.
In my **40 Days** God gave me a brand new
professional keyboard even bigger and better
than the one I asked for.

A.N.

I asked God to give me three more hours
of work a week at the hospital.
God not only gave me the extra hours
but also gave me a better payment.

T.G.

I needed a job, and in my **40 Days**
God gave me two jobs.
I have already paid off one of my debts.

R.M.

Day 25
Be Angry and Sin Not

Be ye angry, and sin not: let not the sun go down upon
your wrath: Neither give place to the devil.

EPHESIANS 4:26-27

STRIFE IS A STRUGGLE FOR VICTORY. When conflict or contention arises in your life, your focus should not be on whether you are right, but that God is right. His purpose must always be a priority in your life.

Strife is sometimes inevitable. When it does arise, deal with it immediately. James 3:16 says that strife opens the door for every evil work. When strife arises, if possible, go back to the exact place where the conflict first occurred. For me there is an added sense of victory if I can overcome the enemy on the same ground where he defeated me. In that place, repent of anything you did that contributed to the strife. Then as we discussed in Day 12, speak death to the crop of dissension you sowed.

If you will consistently deal in this manner with all strife that occurs in your life, you will begin to see the peace of God that passes all understanding become the standard of your lifestyle.

Do not allow strife to come into your marriage, family, home or business. The Bible addresses a Godly anger that confronts sin, but today's Scriptures are not talking about that. Rather they refer to anger that produces strife, bitterness, deceitfulness and things that are intended to hurt another person. Any anger that outlasts the day becomes sin to you. Wisdom dictates that you "choose your battles." Many small issues that should never be addressed in the first place often become huge disputes. As the old adage says, "It takes two to tangle." When strife raises its ugly head, simply choose to humble yourself and be silent.

Check the boxes that indicate where you are:

Ungrateful people
☐ Anger me   ☐ Frustrate me   ☐ Don't make me angry

Gossiping people
☐ Anger me   ☐ Frustrate me   ☐ Don't make me angry

Stingy people
☐ Anger me   ☐ Frustrate me   ☐ Don't make me angry

Controlling people
☐ Anger me   ☐ Frustrate me   ☐ Don't make me angry

Deceitful people
☐ Anger me   ☐ Frustrate me   ☐ Don't make me angry

No one can make you angry. If you are angry, it is because you have chosen to be angry and because a root of anger is already resident in you. Refuse to react when you are provoked; instead, respond as Jesus did. Take this advice from the Book of James:

Wherefore, my beloved brethren, let every man be swift to hear, slow to speak, slow to wrath. JAMES 1:19

Now, underline the actions in the above Scripture that are hardest for you.

❖ *Prayer for the Journey* ❖

FATHER, help me to be a quick and attentive
listener, slow to speak and slow to anger.
Help me to keep thoughts of bitterness
and revenge far from me.
In Jesus' name, *Amen.*

No man ever prayed heartily without learning something.

RALPH WALDO EMERSON

Day 25
Be Angry and Sin Not

"Prayer is More Important"

_____

_____

_____

_____

_____

_____

_____

_____

_____

_____

_____

_____

_____

Remember To Record Your Praise Reports.

Day 26
Learn From Life's Trials

It is good for me that I have been afflicted;
that I might learn thy statutes.

PSALM 119:71

THERE ARE GOING TO BE difficult things that come your way. Sometimes, you bring them on yourself, and sometimes, God allows them. Regardless of the source, you need to learn to grow from every disappointment and heartache. Don't waste your afflictions. Refuse to experience afflictions without learning something from them. You don't want to revisit the same mountains of pain, failure and anguish again and again. Ask the Lord to help you learn from every affliction you encounter.

Today's Scripture says that our afflictions teach us the statutes of the Lord. Literally, statutes are the engraved laws of God. Your trials and afflictions are the very tools the Lord uses to imprint His laws upon your heart.

In Matthew 5:17 Jesus says that He came not to destroy the law but to fulfill it. If you yield to the workings of the Holy Spirit, your afflictions and tribulations will cause the fulfilled law of God to become permanently marked upon your heart, enabling you to grow in your relationship with Him.

Your natural tendency is to ask God to deliver you from everything that is uncomfortable. Unfortunately, the only way you will ever become an overcomer is to have difficulties to overcome. Whenever you face tribulation, testing or persecution, ask the Lord to reveal His purpose for allowing those trials in your life.

Psalm 37:23 tells us that God orders the steps of the righteous man, so even your steps through rough and muddy waters have been ordained by the Lord who dearly loves you. God's plan is that all things work together for your ultimate good. Knowing that will help you praise Him even in the midst of great heartache. Continually remind yourself that God's only purpose in your affliction is to give you a future and a hope (JEREMIAH 29:11). Choose to praise Him continually. Complete the following sentences:

A difficulty this past week from which I learned something about the

Lord was _____

_____

A trial that I face right now from which I need to learn is _____

_____

The most important lesson I learned from past tribulation has been __

_____

When facing trials and tribulations, how do you normally respond? Circle any responses that most closely describe you:

WORRY	REJOICE	FEAR
FEEL DEPRESSED	PRAISE GOD	FEEL DEFEATED
FEEL EXCITED	COMPLAIN	FEEL VICTORIOUS

If you do not face trials with a willingness to learn and to grow, those very trials will inhibit your spiritual growth and will impede your ability to learn God's spiritual principles for maturing you as a saint.

When facing personal trials, I find that rehearsing my former victories is one way that consistently gives me both the faith to endure the trial and the assurance that God will surely bring me through to victory once again.

❖ *Prayer for the Journey* ❖

FATHER, in my life's trials and tribulations teach me every lesson
You have for me to learn. Let me never waste my afflictions on
self-pity or fear. In Jesus' name, *Amen.*

*Promises
are given,
not to supercede,
but to quicken
and encourage
prayer.*

MATTHEW HENRY

Day 26
Learn From Life's Trials

JOURNAL

"Prayer is More Important"

_____

_____

_____

_____

_____

_____

_____

_____

_____

_____

_____

Day 27
Commit to the Lord

Commit thy way unto the LORD;
trust also in him; and he
shall bring it to pass.

PSALM 37:5

WHEN YOU COMMIT YOUR LIFE to the Lord, you attach yourself to Him totally. The Hebrew word for "commit" literally means to "roll yourself up" with God. When you commit your life to Christ, He desires that you release everything that concerns you into His hands. Undeniably, He longs for you to become wrapped up in Him, bound to Him. To trust the Lord means to have complete and bold confidence and reliance upon Him.

What are your priorities in life? Check those things that you are most attached to:

☐ House
☐ Car
☐ Job
☐ Family
☐ Spouse
☐ Money
☐ Success
☐ A relationship
☐ Fame
☐ Education
☐ Power
☐ A friend
☐ Jesus
☐ Other _____

Whatever you commit yourself to, you are "rolled up with," and that pledge can potentially be for life. You must carefully evaluate every commitment *before* you make it.

> *Lay not up for yourselves treasures upon earth, where moth and rust doth corrupt, and where thieves break through and steal: but lay up for yourselves treasures in heaven, where neither moth nor rust doth corrupt, and where thieves do not break in nor steal: for where your treasure is, there will be your heart also.* MATTHEW 6:19-21

Have you committed yourself to eternal things in Christ Jesus, or is your treasure in the fading and temporal things of this world? Commitment to God causes His will to come to pass. If you are genuinely surrendered to the Lord, you can trust that He is going to bring His purposes to fulfillment in your life. Committing these **40 Days** to the Lord will build your faith in Him.

True commitment will build your trust and faith in Christ.

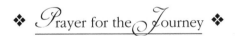

❖ *Prayer for the Journey* ❖

FATHER, please give me the grace and understanding
to commit my life fully to You. I trust You to order
my steps today. In Jesus' name, *Amen.*

Prayer is a strong wall and fortress of the church. It is a goodly Christian weapon.

MARTIN LUTHER

Day 27
Commit to the Lord

"Prayer is More Important"

_____

_____

_____

_____

_____

_____

_____

_____

_____

_____

_____

_____

_____

_____

_____

Day 28
God Will Finish What
He Has Started

*Being confident of this very thing, that he which hath begun a
good work in you will perform it until the day of Jesus Christ.*

PHILIPPIANS 1:6

*For we are made partakers of Christ, if we hold the
beginning of our confidence steadfast unto the end.*

HEBREWS 3:14

AS YOU CONTINUE on your journey through these **40 Days**, it
will be helpful to remember these words of promise. What God
starts, He always finishes. In fact, the Lord has already completed all things because He is the Alpha and the Omega, the beginning and
the end.

What has God begun in your life?

List three new things that God has started in your life recently:

1. _____

2. _____

3. _____

You can trust God to complete what He has begun in your life. Praise
Him now for what He is doing in you during your **40 Days**.

I am reminded of many families with children that are now in their latter
teenage and adult years who have strayed away from the godly principles
they were taught in their youth. If that is your situation, or is the circumstance of someone you love, you can stand on today's Scriptures for these chil-

dren and be assured that God, who began a good work in them, will finish it. God is always faithful to His promise and to His Word.

Acts 16:14 tells us that the Lord opened the heart of Lydia to respond to the words spoken by Paul. As you pray, God will open the hearts of the wayward ones and send seasoned laborers into their paths so that they might once again respond to His love.

❖ *Praise for the Journey* ❖
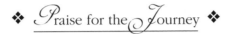

JESUS, thank You for what You are doing in my life.

I am confident that You will personally complete

every good work You have begun in me.

Help me to remain steadfast in that confidence. *Amen.*

Prayer moves the arm, which moves the world, and brings salvation down.

JAMES MONTGOMERY

Day 28
God Will Finish What He Has Started

J O U R N A L

"Prayer is More Important"

_____

_____

_____

_____

_____

_____

_____

_____

_____

_____

_____

_____

Day 29
He Shall Direct Your Paths

In all thy ways acknowledge him,
and he shall direct thy paths.

PROVERBS 3:6

THE LORD ALONE IS GUIDING and directing you through these **40 Days** of prayer. Continue to give Him permission to be a co-partner with you in this covenant time. It is very important that you do not rely upon your natural senses or lean to your own natural logic, but that you trust the Lord during this time.

Your natural senses, education and experiences are valuable gifts from God, but you cannot depend upon them to direct your life. They can be great tools, but were never intended to be used as a compass. True disciples of Jesus allow the Word of God and the Holy Spirit to determine the course their lives will take. Ask the Lord to reveal His plan for your life. He has something very specific He wants you to do. Once you know what that plan is, God will use your natural abilities and past experiences to help you along the way. You should allow God, and God alone to chart the course for your life. It is only in the center of His plan that you can find true peace and fulfillment.

Jesus sent His Holy Spirit to guide our way. Read the following Scriptures, and underline how His Spirit directs our paths:

Nevertheless I tell you the truth; it is expedient for you that I go away:
for if I go not away, the Comforter will not come unto you; but if I depart,
I will send him unto you. And when he is come, he will reprove the world
of sin, and of righteousness, and of judgment: Of sin, because they believe
not on me; of righteousness, because I go to my Father, and ye see me
no more; of judgment, because the prince of this world is judged. I have

yet many things to say unto you, but ye cannot bear them now. Howbeit when he, the Spirit of truth, is come, he will guide you into all truth: for he shall not speak of himself; but whatsoever he shall hear, that shall he speak: and he will shew you things to come. He shall glorify me: for he shall receive of mine, and shall shew it unto you. All things that the Father hath are mine: therefore said I, that he shall take of mine, and shall shew it unto you. JOHN 16:7-15

God's ways are bigger than our ways, and His thoughts are higher than our thoughts. We must be willing to lay aside our own natural understanding. How is the Holy Spirit guiding your way today?

_____

_____

_____

_____

_____

❖ *Prayer for the Journey* ❖

LORD, in the name of Jesus, I ask that Your Holy Spirit
guide and direct all of my ways today. Teach me
Your truth, and give me the grace to lean not
unto my own understanding, *Amen.*

Prayer is not a monologue, but a dialogue; God's voice in response to mine is its most essential part. Listening to God's voice is the secret of the assurance that He will listen to mine.

ANDREW MURRAY

Day 29
He Shall Direct Your Paths

J O U R N A L

"Prayer is More Important"

Day 30
Satisfy Your Hunger and Thirst

And Jesus said unto them, I am the bread of life:
he that cometh to me shall never hunger; and he that
believeth on me shall never thirst.

JOHN 6:35

THE WORD OF GOD is the bread of life. It is important during this covenant time that you are consistently reading your Bible. The best prayer that we can ever pray is the Word of God. As you are going through this **40 Days**, again I encourage you to not only read the Scriptures for each day, but to also use them in your prayers.

Just as your natural man needs natural food to survive, your spiritual man needs spiritual food to survive. Think about this. If a baby refuses to eat, what is the first conclusion its mother will come to? She will conclude that her baby is sick. It's the same way in the things of the spirit. The Word of God is your spiritual food. You will be weak and sick spiritually if you do not eat your food. Your spirit man hungers for the bread of life. Please read the following Scriptures and underline the portions that are nourishing to you.

Thy word have I hid in mine heart, that I might not sin against thee. PSALM 119:11

But his delight is in the law of the LORD; and in his law doth he meditate day and night. PSALM 1:2

This book of the law shall not depart out of thy mouth; but thou shalt meditate therein day and night, that thou mayest observe to do according to all that is written therein: for then thou shalt make thy way prosperous, and then thou shalt have good success. JOSHUA 1:8

Let the word of Christ dwell in you richly in all wisdom; teaching and

admonishing one another in psalms and hymns and spiritual songs,
singing with grace in your hearts to the Lord. COLOSSIANS 3:16

Through prayer, study, meditation, speaking the Word of God and hiding it in your heart, you will feed on the bread of life throughout these **40 Days**. As you feed on God's Word, you will also drink of His living water and will not thirst again. Experience the truth of Jesus' words to the woman at the well:

Whosoever drinketh of this water shall thirst again: But whosoever
drinketh of the water that I shall give him shall never thirst; but the water
that I shall give him shall be in him a well of water springing up into
everlasting life. JOHN 4:13-14

Make a quality decision today to read your Bible daily. Allow the living Word of God to take root in you. Spend time meditating upon it. Fill your mind and mouth with the Scriptures, and you can expect to see answers to your prayers.

❖ *Prayer for the Journey* ❖

LORD, please increase my desire to feed on the bread
of life from Your Word and to drink of Your living water
that I may never thirst again! In Jesus' name, *Amen.*

From morning to night we should think to be too long to be without meat; yet who thinks it is too long to be without prayer?

MATTHEW HENRY

Day 30
Satisfy Your Hunger and Thirst

"Prayer is More Important"

_____

_____

_____

_____

_____

_____

_____

_____

_____

_____

_____

_____

_____

_____

Day 31
Binding and Loosing

Verily I say unto you, Whatsoever ye shall bind on earth shall be bound in heaven, and whatsoever ye shall loose on earth shall be loosed in heaven.

MATTHEW 18:18

SEVERAL YEARS AGO the Lord opened my understanding to today's Scripture and gave me a life-changing revelation that made a significant difference in my prayer life. I want to briefly share that revelation with you here.

Jesus, the Messiah, was a Jew and was first sent to the Jewish people. In Biblical days everyone was classified as either Jew or non-Jew (Gentile). As a Jew, ministering to the Jewish people, Jesus spoke in terms that were very common in that day. The Jewish people studied the teachings of Moses in their Temple, and in Matthew 18:18 Jesus refers to an instruction Moses had taught their forefathers. That instruction was very familiar to everyone listening. I believe that Jesus' audience had no question in their minds concerning what He meant.

Let's look together at Deuteronomy 6:6-9 to see the instruction God the Father had given the children of Israel through His prophet Moses.

And these words, which I command thee this day, shall be in thine heart: And thou shalt teach them unto thy children, and shalt talk of them when thou sittest in thine house, and when thou walkest by the way, and when thou liest down, and when thou risest up. And thou shalt bind them for a sign upon thine hand, and they shall be as frontlets between thy eyes. And thou shalt write them on the posts of thy house and on thy gates.

Jesus told His listeners to do as their forefathers had done and to bind the Word of Almighty God to every person and to every circumstance in their life. Then, what would they loose? They would loose the opposite, everything that did not line up with what the Father had commanded them.

I have been taught binding and loosing principles in church ever since I was a little girl, and never learned these truths the way I now know them. The Holy Spirit, my friend Liberty Savard through her book *Shattering Your Strongholds,* and my Jewish assistant, Linda Markowitz, have all imparted great revelation into my life on the truths of binding and loosing. How simple and easy this principle truly is. Now, I never have any confusion on how to pray as Jesus instructed. As I am led by the Holy Spirit, I bind specific Scriptures to the individuals I am praying for, and I loose them from the bondages of captivity and destruction.

What a powerful key this is! I have written a booklet that explains these key principles more thoroughly. It is a valuable prayer tool. If you would like more information on "Binding and Loosing," I encourage you to get this booklet. You will find ordering instructions in the back of this book.

Let's make what we've learned today very practical. Right now think of one person in your life who is being deceived by the enemy, and pray this prayer:

❖ *Prayer for the Journey* ❖

FATHER, I bring _____ before You today, and I bind
him/her to righteousness, peace and joy in the Holy Ghost.
I bind his/her mind to the mind that is in Christ Jesus, and I say that
_____ will think clearly and be able to see the truth that will
set him/her free. I loose _____ from all lying spirits and
deceiving voices. I ask You, Lord, to bring seasoned laborers
into _____ 's path to minister the truth and life of Jesus.
In His name I pray, *Amen.*

*As we are
involved in
unceasing thinking,
so we are called to
unceasing prayer.*

HENRI NOUWEN

Day 31
Binding and Loosing

J O U R N A L

"Prayer is More Important"

_____

_____

_____

_____

_____

_____

_____

_____

_____

_____

_____

_____

_____

Day 32
Lean Not on Your Own Understanding

*Trust in the LORD with all thine heart; and
lean not unto thine own understanding.*

PROVERBS 3:5

URING THESE **40 DAYS**, it is important that you not lean unto your own understanding or even completely trust what you see or hear. Your five natural senses—sight, sound, touch, smell and taste—are instruments of your body and soul realms. They help you connect with people and natural things, yet are often used by the enemy to distract you from clearly hearing the Spirit of the Lord. Anything that comes from your natural intellect, freewill choice or emotions must be carefully balanced with the Word of God and not irresponsibly attributed to the Holy Spirit. Put an "x" on each line indicating the level of your trust:

I trust what I see

Very little   Very much

I trust what I hear

Very little   Very much

I trust what others say

Very little   Very much

I trust the Word of God

Very little   Very much

Good judgment goes far beyond natural knowledge or experience. Sound judgment is rooted in what God says. Decide in these **40 Days** to believe God for what He knows, not what you know, and for what He says, not what you say.

Underline the parts of the following verses that mean the most to you:

We having the same spirit of faith, according as it is written, I believed, and therefore have I spoken; we also believe, and therefore speak; knowing that he which raised up the Lord Jesus shall raise up us also by Jesus, and shall present us with you. For all things are for your sakes, that the abundant grace might through the thanksgiving of many redound to the glory of God. For which cause we faint not; but though our outward man perish, yet the inward man is renewed day by day. For our light affliction, which is but for a moment, worketh for us a far more exceeding and eternal weight of glory; while we look not at the things which are seen, but at the things which are not seen: for the things which are seen are temporal; but the things which are not seen are eternal.

II CORINTHIANS 4:13-18

Trust the Lord to give you His knowledge and His good judgment. Choose to believe His Word, and don't lean to your own understanding. God shall, indeed, bring to pass the things He has promised you. Only those who trust God for the invisible will see the impossible done in their lives.

❖ *Prayer for the Journey* ❖

LORD, please fill me with Your wisdom and
understanding. Help me to know and to trust You,
especially when I cannot readily see or hear the
answers that I need. In Jesus' name, *Amen.*

*Do you know
what is wrong with
the world today?
There is too much
theologian and
not enough
kneeologian.*

DALLAS F. BILLINGTON

Day 32
Lean Not on Your Own Understanding

JOURNAL

"Prayer is More Important"

_____

_____

_____

_____

_____

_____

_____

_____

_____

_____

_____

_____

_____

Testimonial

During my **40 Days** of prayer my husband
was delivered from alcohol. He had been
drinking for over thirty years. He came to
the watch night service at my church on
New Year's Eve, and not only did he give
his life to the Lord, but he has not had a
drink or even the taste for alcohol since.
He is still in church with me and
is stronger everyday.

N.P.
Florida

Freeda and Prayer Partners, you would not
believe the difference in my son. In my
40 Days he has stopped his party lifestyle,
is thankful to God even for his troubles,
prays all the time and has new goals. He is
also seeking new friends who can help
him reach those goals. God is awesome!

T.D.
Florida

Day 33
Guard Your Tongue

A soft answer turneth away wrath:
but grievous words stir up anger...
A man hath joy by the answer of his mouth,
and a word spoken in due season, how good is it!

PROVERBS 15:1,23

DURING THIS COVENANT TIME you may have an occasion to speak from an anxious or worried heart. If you yield to that temptation, your tongue can become a tool of strife and division. It is important that you are faithful in turning away from every form of wrath, strife and grievous words. You must diligently forbid anger to stir within you or to rise up in your household.

Read each of the following verses and jot down what they say about anger:

Proverbs 15:18 _____

_____

_____

Ephesians 4:26 _____

_____

_____

James 1:19 _____

_____

_____

These Scriptures help you to see that you have joy by the answer of your mouth, and that the word fitly spoken in due season is good. You must guard the words of your mouth every day, but especially during this covenant time with the Lord. Ask Him to help you to resist all anger and strife.

An ancient Chinese proverb says:

Three gatekeepers are commanded to halt
and ask a question of every word
that passes through your mouth.

If the word cannot answer "yes" to each question,
It cannot proceed.

The first gatekeeper will ask, "Is it true?"
The second gatekeeper will ask, "Is it kind?"
The third gatekeeper will ask, "Is it necessary?"

What truth! If each of us would only speak the things that are true, kind and necessary, how peaceful our world would be. Of course, I'm speaking idealistically, but you and I can surely do our part. If every word we speak can get past these gatekeepers, we can expect great change in our personal lives, in our homes, and in everything that concerns us.

If you have been angry with someone, ask both the Lord and that person to forgive you. The bigger person is the one who says "I'm sorry" first.

❖ 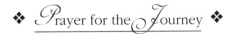 *Prayer for the Journey* ❖

ALMIGHTY GOD, in the name of Jesus, please
put a guard over my lips that my words may never be used as
a tool of strife in the hands of the enemy, Amen.

What answers to prayer have I been unable to see because I am not in close enough communion with God?

OSWALD CHAMBERS

Day 33
Guard Your Tongue

JOURNAL

"Prayer is More Important"

_____

_____

_____

_____

_____

_____

_____

_____

_____

_____

_____

_____

Remember To Record Your Praise Reports.

Day 34
Don't Worry!

Be careful for nothing; but in everything
by prayer and supplication with thanksgiving
let your requests be made known unto God.

PHILIPPIANS 4:6

E STEADFAST IN PRAYER. Remember to pray persistently and continually. You have much to accomplish in this committed time of prayer. During these **40 Days** you may discover that you have new needs arise. Don't worry, and don't start over! This is a covenant time dedicated to your Lord. Just add the new needs to your prayer list and continue in your journey. This is not to be a time of bondage but a time of sweet fellowship with God.

The new needs that have surfaced in these **40 Days** include the following:

1. _____

2. _____

3. _____

Also, as you pray, remember to be thankful to God for the little things in your life. Refuse to be concerned about the new needs you have. Thank the Lord for the abundance He has already given you, and be especially thankful for the privilege of bringing everything to Him in prayer. Communion with God is your highest privilege.

Sometimes, God may delay the answers to your prayers because you have not been grateful for what you have already been given. The Word tells us that we enter into His gates with thanksgiving and into His courts with praise (PSALM 100:4). You can't even get past the gates of His presence without a thankful heart filled with praise.

God uses His Word to build our faith but requires praise to release that faith to bring answers we are believing for.

Check your heart. Are you thankful? Prioritize from the most thankful (1) to the least thankful (7) the list below:

_____ Family

_____ Spouse

_____ Children

_____ Financial blessings

_____ Work

_____ Church relationships

_____ Other_____

❖ Praise for the Journey ❖

FATHER, I am so grateful that I can bring any need
to You in prayer. My heart is filled with thanksgiving
for all that You have already given to me. I thank
You, and I praise You for what is yet ahead. Amen.

We honor God when we ask for great things. It is a humiliating thing to think that we are satisfied with very small results.

D. L. MOODY

Day 34
Don't Worry!

J O U R N A L

"Prayer is More Important"

_____

_____

_____

_____

_____

_____

_____

_____

_____

_____

_____

_____

_____

Day 35
Temple Maintenance

Know ye not that ye are the temple of God, and that the Spirit of God dwelleth in you? If any man defile the temple of God, him shall God destroy; for the temple of God is holy, which temple ye are.

I CORINTHIANS 3:16-17

YOUR PHYSICAL BODY is the temple of God, and it carries His Holy presence. It is your responsibility to perform regular "temple maintenance," making sure that your body remains as healthy and strong as God desires it to be.

Check all of the ways that you are taking care of your physical temple:

☐ Proper nutrition with supplements, if necessary
☐ Drinking adequate amounts of water
☐ Prayer
☐ Keeping the Sabbath
☐ Breaking agreement with fear and stress

☐ Regular health checkups
☐ Adequate rest
☐ Regular exercise
☐ Fasting
☐ Staying morally pure
☐ Other:

_____

_____

Today's Scripture says, "If any man defile the temple of God, him shall God destroy." This is a very strong word of admonition. It is essential you understand that your physical body is not yours, but it is the temple of the living God and belongs to Him. You do not have the right to neglect or abuse your physical flesh.

Once while praying for a friend who was facing major life-threatening surgery, I learned how serious God is about this mandate. He said that because my friend had not repented of neglecting her body, He could not move in Divine healing on her behalf. The wages of sin is death, and death was still reigning in my friend's body because she had not repented of neglecting her health. The Lord led me and my prayer partners to pray for a safe and effective surgery for my friend, saying that He would heal her through that means. That is exactly what happened, and my friend is well today. I am so grateful for this powerful lesson I learned about repenting for neglecting my own body.

What changes do you need to make in the care of your physical temple? List the three most important things:

1. _____

2. _____

3. _____

God desires that you live a long and healthy life and be a witness of His love and faithfulness. He desires that you fulfill your destiny in Him, serving Him all the days of your life with a strong, healthy body.

Many sick believers stand in faith for their physical healing even to their death without realizing their need to repent. If you have neglected your body and, as a result, are in poor health, repent to the Lord for defiling His temple. Our physical bodies are entrusted to us to carry the presence of God in the earth. Whatever we willfully do to defile or destroy our body is sin to us and must be repented of.

If we confess our sins, he is faithful and just to forgive us our sins, and to cleanse us from all unrighteousness. I JOHN 1:9

The sins of disobedience that I need to confess concerning the care of my physical body include the following:

_____

å_____

❖ *Praise for the Journey* ❖

FATHER, I give You thanks for my physical body. Grant me Your wisdom to properly care for my temple. Grant that my days may be long upon the earth. I will not fail to praise You for it. Amen.

*I have often
learned more in one
prayer than I have
been able to glean
from much reading
and reflection.*

MARTIN LUTHER

Day 35
Temple Maintenance

JOURNAL

"Prayer is More Important"

Day 36
Spiritual Warfare

For the weapons of our warfare are not carnal,
but mighty through God to the pulling down of strongholds;
casting down imaginations, and every high thing that exalteth itself against
the knowledge of God, and bringing into
captivity every thought to the obedience of Christ.

II CORINTHIANS 10:4-5

For we wrestle not against flesh and blood, but against principalities,
against powers, against the rulers of the darkness of this world,
against spiritual wickedness in high places.

EPHESIANS 6:12

WE ARE AT WAR, but our battle is not against people directly. Let me explain. Perhaps you are asking God to intervene on the behalf of someone, maybe a member of your family or someone that you love, and you can clearly see that there are things not right in his or her life. To pray effectively, you must separate the sin from the sinner. As today's Scripture says, do not fight against flesh and blood, which is the person, but instead withhold the rulers of darkness and enforce the victory that Jesus has already won. In other words, fight against the sin, not against the sinner.

Another area of spiritual warfare often comes from within. Romans 8:7 says that our carnal mind is at enmity against God. It is a battle to embrace the truth. That is, you must make an aggressive and consistent effort to cast down every vain imagination and take every thought captive and allow both your heart and mind to be filled with the Word of God. Don't allow satan to deceive you into sacrificing the glory of God in your life for a few moments of self-indulgence and sin.

Circle the thoughts that are most difficult for you to take captive:

GREEDY THOUGHTS   ANGRY THOUGHTS

LUSTFUL THOUGHTS   DEPRESSED THOUGHTS

VAIN THOUGHTS   ANXIOUS THOUGHTS

IMPATIENT THOUGHTS

Other _____

❖ *Prayer for the Journey* ❖

LORD, help me to recognize and to cast down
every vain imagination and to take every thought
captive that would exalt itself higher than you in my life.
Help me to separate the sin from the sinner
as I pray for others. In Jesus' name, Amen.

Beware in your prayer, above everything, of limiting God, not only by unbelief, but by fancying that you know what He can do.

ANDREW MURRAY

Day 36
Spiritual Warfare

JOURNAL

"Prayer is More Important"

_____

_____

_____

_____

_____

_____

_____

_____

_____

_____

_____

_____

Day 37
God Is Able

For the which cause I also suffer these things: nevertheless
I am not ashamed: for I know whom I have believed,
and am persuaded that he is able to keep that which
I have committed unto him against that day.

II TIMOTHY 1: 12

Now unto him that is able to do exceedingly abundantly
above all that we ask or think, according to the
power that worketh within us.

EPHESIANS 3:20

BOTH OF THESE VERSES, and especially the last one, have powerful messages. There is no prayer so big that God can't answer. Think about that. What is the biggest need you have been praying for? Even if it seems overwhelming to you, God can handle your biggest need. It is a very small matter to Him.

In fact, God is more than able, not only to keep what you have committed unto Him during this time, but He is surely able to bring His Divine intervention into your every situation. No matter how things look in the natural, God is able to do far more than you can think or ask.

During these **40 Days**, you have a covenant with God for several requests. You are praying that the Father reveal His heart concerning your every need, and you are listening as He instructs you through His Holy Spirit. As a result, your faith is growing stronger as you witness God's faithfulness to meet your every need.

Complete each of the following sentences:

In my family, I am trusting God to _____

_____

_____

In my marriage, I am trusting God to _____

_____

_____

In my work, I am trusting God to _____

_____

_____

At my church, I am trusting God to _____

_____

_____

❖ *Prayer for the Journey* ❖

FATHER, You are able to meet every need and to
overcome every obstacle in my life. I trust You to
keep all that You have promised to me until that perfect
day and time when You will be glorified in my life.
In Jesus' name, Amen.

*Pray the
largest prayers.
You cannot think
a prayer so large
that God, in
answering it,
will not wish you
had made it larger.
Pray not for crutches
but for wings!*

PHILLIPS BROOKS

Day 37
God Is Able

JOURNAL

"Prayer is More Important"

_____

_____

_____

_____

_____

_____

_____

_____

_____

_____

_____

_____

_____

Day 38
Rightly Divide the Truth

Study to shew thyself approved unto God,
a workman that needeth not to be ashamed,
rightly dividing the word of truth....
All scripture is given by inspiration of God,
and is profitable for doctrine, for reproof, for correction,
for instruction in righteousness.

II TIMOTHY 2:15; 3:16

BY NOW, you should have developed a regular time each day to be with God, to study His Word and to pray. It is my desire that this 40-Day journal will help you develop a lifelong habit of prayer and studying your Bible.

As you hear the Father's heart in your prayer time, you can always confirm what you hear by the Bible. God's revealed Word never contradicts His written Word.

It is important that you know the Scriptures well. In order to study God's Word effectively, you need to do the following (check the ones you are already doing):

☐ Have a good translation of the Bible that you understand.
☐ Read a passage thoroughly two or three times aloud.
☐ Study the notes from a study Bible or good Bible commentary.
☐ Memorize the Scriptures.
☐ Look at the entire context of your passage.
☐ Study the Word with other Christians.
☐ Use a concordance to look up other key passages.
☐ Use a Bible dictionary to enlarge your understanding.

I often use the Scriptures to "chase" God's revealed word to me. For instance, when God speaks His Word to my heart, I will quickly find a passage to support what I've heard and then will use a good Bible concordance to locate other related Scriptures. Many times, I discover the answer to my need as I search the Scriptures and expand on what I originally heard from the Holy Spirit. Because God's Word always gives life, make it the life-source of your prayer life. The answer to every need in life can be met through embracing the Holy Scriptures.

The Holy Spirit will teach you truth and give you beneficial inspiration for your own life. Ask the Holy Spirit to speak to you through the Scriptures. Spend time in your Bible and become very familiar with its wealth. If you are intimately acquainted with the genuine, you will never be deceived by the counterfeit.

And ye shall know the truth, and the truth shall make you free. JOHN 8:32

❖ 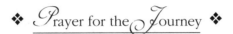 ❖

FATHER, enable me to interpret the Word
that You have for me each day. Show me how to
rightly divide everything I hear
and how to apply it to my life.
In Jesus' name, Amen.

*Don't allow yourself
to be burdened by any
one form of prayer.
Don't tie yourself to
repetition or set form.
Simply engage in
conversation with the
One who adores you
unconditionally.*

MADAME GUYON

Day 38
Rightly Divide the Truth

JOURNAL

"Prayer is More Important"

_____

_____

_____

_____

_____

_____

_____

_____

_____

_____

_____

_____

Day 39
The Power of the Holy Spirit

But ye shall receive power, after that the Holy Ghost
is come upon you: and ye shall be witnesses unto me
both in Jerusalem, and in all Judaea, and in Samaria,
and unto the uttermost part of the earth.

ACTS 1: 8

WE RECEIVE THE HOLY SPIRIT at the time of our salvation. It is through the Holy Spirit that we become one with Christ, but there is a subsequent experience with the Holy Spirit that enables us to access the power of God in our lives. That experience is given as a gift to those who ask for it in faith. This gift is known as the baptism of the Holy Spirit and it comes with the evidence of speaking in tongues. The gift of tongues gives you the ability to pray in a language you do not know. Praying in tongues does many things. It opens doors that cannot be opened any other way. Jude 20 tells us that praying in the Spirit builds us up on our most holy faith.

The baptism of the Holy Spirit is a gift from God. All you must do to receive it is, first, be born again, then ask the Father in Jesus' name to give you this glorious gift. God is no respecter of persons; you will not be denied.

Read the Scriptures below and underline the demonstrations of the power of the Holy Spirit that manifested in the early church.

And he said unto them, Go ye into all the world, and preach the gospel to every creature. He that believeth and is baptized shall be saved; but he that believeth not shall be damned. And these signs shall follow them that believe; In my name shall they cast out devils; they shall speak with new tongues; they shall take up serpents; and if they drink any deadly thing, it shall not hurt them; they shall lay hands on the sick, and they shall recover. MARK 16:15-18

And suddenly there came a sound from heaven as of a rushing mighty wind, and it filled all the house where they were sitting. And there appeared unto them cloven tongues like as of fire, and it sat upon each of them. And they were all filled with the Holy Ghost, and began to speak with other tongues, as the Spirit gave them utterance. ACTS 2:2-4

While Peter yet spake these words, the Holy Ghost fell on all them which heard the word. And they of the circumcision which believed were astonished, as many as came with Peter, because that on the Gentiles also was poured out the gift of the Holy Ghost. For they heard them speak with tongues, and magnify God. Then answered Peter, Can any man forbid water, that these should not be baptized, which have received the Holy Ghost as well as we? ACTS 10:44-47

This realm of power in the Holy Spirit enables you to operate in the supernatural strength of God. It will help you become an effective witness to your family, to your community and to the uttermost parts of the earth.

❖ *Prayer for the Journey* ❖

FATHER, I ask in the name of Your Son Jesus
that You baptize me with the Holy Spirit.
Fill me with the power to witness
to others the good news of the gospel, Amen.

Praying in tongues is the God within me speaking to Himself, allowing me to participate in Heavenly transactions. What an honor!

FREEDA BOWERS

Day 39
The Power of the Holy Spirit

JOURNAL

"Prayer is More Important"

_____

_____

_____

_____

_____

_____

_____

_____

_____

_____

_____

_____

Day 40
There Is More

*But as it is written, Eye hath not seen, nor ear heard,
neither have entered into the heart of man, the things
which God hath prepared for them that love him.
But God hath revealed them unto us by his Spirit:
for the Spirit searcheth all things,
yea, the deep things of God.*

I CORINTHIANS 2:9-10

MUCH LIES BEYOND TODAY. You have received far more in these **40 Days** than your natural reasoning understands. Actually, the human mind does not have the ability to comprehend what has transpired during this covenant time with God. Your commitment to this journey has released covenant revelation in your heart. That revelation is like a seed growing. Though in some cases you may not yet see the evidence of the things you have believed for, your prayers are still doing their work and will take on a tangible form in the days and months ahead. You can rest in knowing that the Holy Spirit is constantly working on your behalf to bring you all of the things you need to live a peaceful and victorious life.

Today's verse tells us that the Holy Spirit searches the deep things of God. As you continue to trust the Lord and maintain your mindset of faith concerning the things you have prayed for, He will be faithful to locate those answers and bring them to you.

Complete these sentences:

The most exciting answer to prayer during this **40 Days** has been

_____

_____

The most significant insight into God's Word I received during this **40 Days** has been_____

_____

_____

One important way God changed me during these **40 Days** has been

_____

_____

Congratulations! You have finished this portion of the race. I commend you for your faithfulness and rejoice with you over every answered prayer. I encourage you to continue giving God 40 minutes every day, expecting great impartations and revelations all along your journey.

This is not the end of your journey with God, only the beginning of a deeper walk with Him. I trust that this is not the last **40 Days** you will consecrate to God, but will become the first of many. This is not the culmination of seeing Him answer your prayers, it is an initial testimony and witness to you that God is faithful and able to supply all your needs through His riches in glory in Christ Jesus.

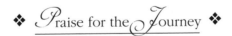

❖ *Praise for the Journey* ❖

THANK YOU, LORD, for meeting with me in these **40 Days**.

I praise You for answered prayer, and I give You glory

for making it very real to me that

Prayer is More Important.

Amen.

*He who
ceases to pray
ceases to prosper.*

❧

<small>SIR WILLIAM GURNEY BENHAM</small>

Day 40
There Is More

JOURNAL

"Prayer is More Important"

_____

_____

_____

_____

_____

_____

_____

_____

_____

_____

_____

_____

Testimonial

Freeda, when you first shared with me the 40-Day Plan several years ago, my initial thoughts went something like this: "Whoa! 40 minutes a day for **40 Days**! What can I say in 40 minutes?" Over the years I've had lots to say…to my husband…my children…my friends…and my students, but regrettably, I had little to say to God. Ever so often I talked to Him—when I had a need—but the idea of getting alone with God for any extended period of time—secluded from my family and my books—was not that appealing to me…then. Yet, when you shared the plan with me that day years ago, there was something about your revelation that spoke life to my spirit, and I knew this was for me.

Since that time, I have done the **40 Days** on several occasions for a number of needs and wants. With each time, I've experienced God's love, grace and mercy as He made Himself so real in my life. With each time, I've witnessed God's benevolence and power as He met my needs— needs that, at times, seemed impossible to meet. As a result of this time with the Lord, I've developed a love and desire for His presence, unlike anything I've ever known. As a result of this time with Him, I've learned how to submit and trust in who He is and what He is. As a result of my obedience, I have learned how to touch His heart. As a result of this time with Him, I've truly learned how to pray—to talk to God—to commune with Him on a daily basis. I conclude as a result of my spiritual growth that the 40-Day Plan has been my avenue to a closer and higher walk with the Lord.

I have grown in God, and now I find that 40 minutes a day isn't always enough. So, I've been getting up at 4:30 A.M. to allow myself time in His presence.

S.J.
Florida

esources

For additional resources by Freeda Bowers
or to contact her to speak at your next event, please write or call:

Freeda Bowers Ministries
P.O. Box 608752
Orlando, FL 32860
For bookings & product order only,
call 1-877-409-4040.
For additional inquiries,
call 407-862-0740.

E-Mail: freeda@freedabowers.com
Web Page: http://www.freedabowers.com

Give Me 40 Days for Healing

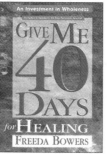

■ Do you need a manifestation of God's healing power in your life? Total health is a part of every believer's covenant with God, but it will not come to you automatically. Every Christian must learn how to apprehend healing. This book is a great coach to teach you how to obtain Divine health and wholeness for every area of your life. *Hardcover book.*

Binding and Loosing

■ An illuminating teaching based upon the instructions of Jesus found in Matthew 16:19 and 18:18. There has been a great deal of confusion and controversy about what Jesus refers to in these passages. In this teaching Freeda gives a clear and concise understanding from the Scriptures of what Jesus imparts to His followers. Freeda shows how to effectively pray powerful "binding and loosing" prayers using as samples some prayers for the most common problems facing mankind today. *Booklet and two CDs in an album.*

Over My Dead Body

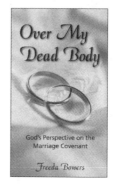

■ A vital message on the marriage covenant. God's will that marriage be forever is viewed through His eyes as Freeda takes you through the Scriptures teaching God's intended purpose for the marriage union, revealing how we often fall far short of the joy available to us. *Booklet.*

Generational Repentance

■ An enlightening teaching on destroying genera-

tional curses. Many families are plagued generation after generation with besetting sin and destructive addictive behaviors. Co-teaching with her personal assistant Linda Markowitz, Freeda exposes the root of generational captivity and gives the tools necessary to set the captives free. *Booklet and two CDs in an album.*

Where is Your Heart?

■ Freeda exposes one of the greatest tools of the enemy. You can be doing all of the "right" things, but with a wrong heart motive and sadly find your efforts burned as wood, hay and stubble on the Day of Judgment. The Lord looks upon our heart, and this wonderful teaching reveals the necessity of examining your own. *Booklet.*

Secrets to Prevailing Prayer

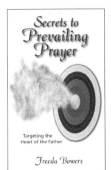

■ David prayed prayers that prevailed against enormous obstacles and is the only person recorded in the Bible to have the heart of God. What did David know that perhaps we have missed? In this insightful teaching Freeda gives five wonderful prayer keys that could become the five smooth stones you need to overcome the Goliaths in your life. *Booklet.*

Notes

Notes

Notes

Notes

Notes

Notes

Notes